T0209488

The King Said:
Learn from Me

Dr. Walter Koch

WESTBOW
PRESS®
A DIVISION OF THOMAS NELSON
& ZONDERVAN

THE HOLY BIBLE, NEW INTERNATIONAL VERSION®, NIV® Copyright © 1973, 1978, 1984, 2011 by Biblica, Inc.® Used by permission. All rights reserved worldwide.

Scripture taken from the New King James Version®. Copyright © 1982 by Thomas Nelson. Used by permission. All rights reserved.

Scripture taken from the King James Version of the Bible.

WestBow Press books may be ordered through booksellers or by contacting:

WestBow Press
A Division of Thomas Nelson & Zondervan
1663 Liberty Drive
Bloomington, IN 47403
www.westbowpress.com
1 (866) 928-1240

ISBN: 978-1-9736-5246-5 (sc)
ISBN: 978-1-9736-5247-2 (e)

Print information available on the last page.

WestBow Press rev. date: 02/11/2019

The King Said:
Learn from Me

DEDICATION

I dedicate this book to my lovely wife, Raquel, whom I married in 1977. She has made me a proud father to our son, Ruben William. She is my partner whom I love, the one who is always by my side, and who also shines in her God-given gifts to teach the Word of God and to help women discover their purpose and potential in the Kingdom.

To my son, Ruben William, who also encouraged me to write this book. He is an inspiration to me. My wife and I acknowledge the Lord's calling on his life to teach Kingdom principles.

To my late parents, Juan and Luba, for giving me life so I could fulfill my purpose on this Earth. To Pedro, Jose, Regina, Ruben, and Rosa (my brothers and sisters), and their families. To my in-laws, Gregorio and Nidia, who have shown great support for my calling.

To our dear congregation, Centro Diplomático Internacional in El Monte, California, where my wife and I have served as Pastors since 1982. It is there that we strive to be a blessing to God's people and teach revelations of His word—to nurture, develop, and elevate their thinking to attain the mind of Christ who lives in them. To all the workers in each department that help the ministry function with excellence. A very special dedication and thanks to our leaders who assist us in every area of ministry: Tony and Rosa Perez, and their son, Joe; Gerson and Randy Martinez, and their children, Matthew and Jackie; Jacob and Dena Baca, and their son Jakey, whom we embrace as our grandson; Edgar and Leann Murillo, and their daughter Olivia, whom we embrace as our granddaughter; my older brother and his wife, Pedro and Susan Tkaez, and their son, Javier; our personal assistant and office manager, Rosa Magaña, and her husband,

Greg. These ministers are God's gift to the Kingdom and us. We love them and bless them for their service.

To Enlace (Spanish TBN), its President, Jonas Gonzalez, and the Gonzalez family. At Enlace, I have the privilege of serving as a member of the Board of Directors and have the opportunity to share the Kingdom of God with many nations.

To my dear friend and mentor, the late Dr. Myles Munroe of Bahamas Faith Ministries International (BFMI), and his wife, Ruth. I met Dr. Munroe in 1990 and had the honor of serving as his Spanish language interpreter when we traveled to speak in various countries. I also have the privilege of being a Trustee on the board of the International Third World Leaders Association (ITWLA), which Dr. Munroe and a group of like-minded Kingdom visionaries founded in 1986. To Dr. and Mrs. Munroe's children, Myles Jr. and Charisa, who carry on the legacy of their parents.

To the countless viewers of our international television program **"Diplomatic Vision"** in Spanish. To our many colleagues around the world who have the same passion for teaching the Word of the King. To the ministers and congregations that are under our covering and mentorship in Venezuela, Argentina, and Colombia.

A Special thanks to Pastor Rubén Casas (translator, interpreter, and editor), Dr. Marcelo Laffitte and Jasmine Colbert for editing the book.

To the Creator, our dear God, who one day touched my soul, illuminated my mind, and changed my life when He revealed these words: "Learn from Me." That same message flows through this book today to bless the lives of its readers!

TABLE OF CONTENTS

A SPECIAL DEDICATION TO
DR. MYLES MUNROE

Dr. Myles Munroe was a great champion and teacher of the Kingdom message. I am honored to say that he was my Pastor and a very dear friend. For many years, our church had the privilege of collaborating with his ministries, the BFMI and the ITWLA, to take the Kingdom message worldwide. Dr. Munroe's passing in 2014 was a great loss to the Body of Christ, but he left a legacy of Kingdom teachings that will be a blessing to Believers and the world for many generations to come.

When I began writing this book in 2013, I asked Dr. Munroe if he would write the foreword. After reading the first draft, he not only agreed to write the foreword but also gave me very encouraging feedback. He described the book as "wonderful" and having "great substance." He also made helpful suggestions for improvements. His kind words and advice were invaluable.

I am honored to share the email that Dr. Munroe sent me in 2013. Although I am saddened that I was not able to celebrate the book's completion with him, I will forever be grateful for his guidance and support.

From: myleshumble
To: acokson@aol.com
Sent: 11/27/2012 8:11:08 P.M. Pacific Standard Time
Subj: RE: Dr. Walter Koch BOOK, Learn From Me

Dear Walter my son,

Warm Kingdom Greetings from Orlando where Ruth and I a trying to get a few days break!

I am still enjoying the over flow of the Global Leadership summit which continues to receive hundreds of positive comments from those who attended and joined online. I am grateful to all who made this leadership event such a success. Thank you for your prayers for us.

Thanks for the attached document. I review it and think you have great substance and the content is wonderful.

I have a few suggestion:

I hope this review helps.

Love you,

papa

Dr. Walter Koch with Dr. Myles Munroe

FOREWORD

What could help a man understand the sublime act of giving birth to a child other than writing a book?

The pain of childbirth, the anticipation, and the anxiety before the child arrives are much like the labor of compiling one's thoughts into a cohesive work. The role I have played in this process is like that of a midwife. Helping Dr. Koch with the birth of this book has been extraordinary.

I have assisted the "births" of hundreds of books, so I am not exaggerating when I say that I welcomed Dr. Koch's unique and timely work. The contents are far from the religious and traditional ideas that we are accustomed to; this is no small thing.

It has been a blessing from Heaven to develop a genuine brotherhood and work with a man to whom God has revealed very profound mysteries of the Word, a man so committed to the cause of the Kingdom, and a man so passionate to share his vast wealth of scriptural knowledge. That alone has been a unique and enriching experience as a book publisher. I sincerely thank the author for honoring me with such a privilege.

Dear reader, I invite you to delight yourself in a work that will edify your life and lead you on a most critical journey as a Believer—**Learning from King Jesus.**

Dr. Marcelo Laffitte
Editor

THE KING SAID: "LEARN FROM ME."
By Dr. Walter Koch.

This is a useful apologetics text for anyone who wishes to measure their life experiences against the rubric of the Kingdom of God. It is written in an easy conversational style laced with the practical experiences of the author who was inspired by his mentor, the late Dr. Myles Munroe. Now his reflections find meaningful application as he instructs his own son, Rubén William as well as his congregants, and now his readers.

Central to his arguments are the extensive scripture texts with their pointed teachings and key character references which validate the Kingdom of God. His use of imagery is convincing. Study the "caged bird" exemplifying our enslavement to denominational religion and political government. Picture the "ascending elevator" representing the inspired mind rising to new heights to grasp a panoramic view of reality.

For me, the central thrust of this masterful work comes in his convincing treatment of the Kingdom of God in discovering our purpose in life, our potential to generate productivity and our power to triumph over poverty, to temper fear and emotional anxiety and to manage our physical health.

I read this manuscript through with keen interest so that like Dr. Koch I too might sit at the feet of King Jesus and Learn from Him.

Drs. C.B. Peter and C. Patricia Morgan

Dr. C.B. Peter Morgan
D. Min, M. Div, B.A.
President IAKCM
Myles E. Munroe Diplomat Center
Carmichael Road,
Nassau, Bahamas

Comment/Endorsement

Congratulations, Dr. Walter Koch, for your outstanding book, *The King said Learn from Me*. As I was reading it, I was greatly blessed and I learned much about the very important and necessary lessons you share about our King Jesus and the reality of His Kingdom here on earth. This book is full of powerful advice for everybody, for all Pastors, Ministers, leaders and servants of God. I highly recommend it and I'm sure the reader will be immensely blessed because there is nothing better in life than to continually learn from our King, to know Him, to spend time with Him, to grow in Him, to serve Him and to experience the reality and power of His Kingdom in our lives today, instead of living a limited, unjoyful, and unfruitful life.

I enjoyed your wise teachings found in this book, especially when you expand about the correct interpretation of living as who we are, "Children of God," and "Citizens of His Kingdom." Jesus preached and taught about God's Kingdom on earth, and I agree with you that it should be our message today to a world in disarray needing new life in Christ. This book must be translated in Spanish and in all the languages for the world to understand and to experience the reality and the power of God's Kingdom in their lives today. I encourage everybody to read this book, your life will be changed, and God will use you to transform communities and cities around the world.

Thanks, Dr. Koch, for such a timely and powerful book.

Dr. Sergio Navarrete
Vice-President of the Global Hispanic Assemblies of God Fraternity
Superintendent of the Southern Pacific District
of the Assemblies of God

Comment / Endorsement

My dear friend, Dr. Walter Koch's book *The King Said Learn From Me* is a must read that will gloriously bring the reader back to the feet of Jesus! "The King Said Learn From Me" is a paradigm shift from the Christian experience that headlines the blessings of God to one that first and foremost flows from the love and worship of God from whom all blessings flow. I highly recommend this to all that truly want to learn from Him!

Rev. Greg Mauro
Vice President, Morris Cerullo Ministries
Bedford, TX 76021-5858

PREFACE

Early one morning in 2006, I was in my office studying the Scripture Matthew 11:29:

> *"Take my yoke upon you and learn from me, for I am gentle and humble in heart, and you will find rest for your souls." (New International Version)*

As I meditated, three words in the verse grabbed my attention: **"Learn from Me"**. As I pondered their meaning, I felt a profound sense of urgency. I felt that the Spirit of God was leading me to teach on that verse for more than just one Sunday; He wanted it to be the subject of my sermons for the entire year. So, I did just that. Every Sunday that year, I spoke to our congregation, Centro Diplomático, on King Jesus' words, **"Learn from Me"**.

Each time I taught from Matthew 11:29, I asked God to illuminate me to find the precious pearls contained in the passage. Knowing that the deep mysteries of the Bible are undetectable to those who are in a hurry, I patiently waited in meditation with the Lord so I could absorb all the riches He had hidden in those words. Without fail, the Lord rewarded my patience by revealing the great wisdom and meaning in that verse.

This book does not encompass all the teachings, exhortations, directions, and loving suggestions that Almighty God gave me during that unique experience, but it does provide a comprehensive review of what I learned. I assure you that what I present in this work will be a spiritual feast and tremendous blessing!

My friend, I hope this book inspires you to approach the Word of God with the pick and shovel of Biblical curiosity, that the central message of this work resonates in your heart, and that you will be able to apply its lessons to your daily life. If you do, I am confident God will generously respond to your intense study of His Word with His eternal truths and profound revelations on the process and power of **Learning from King Jesus**.

Dr. Walter Koch

INTRODUCTION
ONE YEAR AT THE FEET OF KING JESUS

When I began my journey to **learn from King Jesus**, I knew I needed to have the correct spiritual posture, perspective, and attitude. I had to make learning from Him my spiritual priority. I needed to dedicate my focus to **Matthew 11:29** so I could grasp all the wisdom that the Lord wanted to reveal. I had to be still and listen to His voice, I had to have a hunger and enthusiasm to **learn from King Jesus** (the Master Teacher), and I had to value the teachings contained in that verse:

> 29 *"Take my yoke upon you and learn from me, for I am gentle and humble in heart, and you will find rest for your souls." (NIV)*

I also knew the Lord's unique request had to become the priority of the congregation at Centro Diplomático. I postponed any sermons I had planned and focused our studies on *learning from Him.*

MAKING THE TEACHINGS OF KING JESUS A PRIORITY

Prioritizing the Lord's assignment to study **Matthew 11:29** reminds me of the story of Mary and her sister, Martha. In **Luke Chapter 10**, the sisters had the privilege of hosting King Jesus as a guest in their home.

Something unusual happened when King Jesus arrived. Martha continued to serve the other guests, but Mary immediately stopped helping her sister so she could sit and listen to King Jesus teach:

> 38 *Now it came to pass, as they went, that he entered into a certain village: and a certain woman named Martha received him into her house.*

39 And she had a sister called Mary, which also sat at Jesus' feet, and heard his word. (Luke 10:38-39)

Martha became angry with Mary because there was still much to do. She even tried to convince King Jesus that Mary was wrong for not helping her:

40 But Martha was cumbered about much serving, and came to him, and said, Lord, dost thou not care that my sister hath left me to serve alone? bid her therefore that she help me. (Luke 10:40)

Rather than scold Mary for not helping Martha, King Jesus did the opposite and applauded Mary's decision:

41 And Jesus answered and said unto her, Martha, Martha, thou art careful and troubled about many things:

42 But one thing is needful: and Mary hath chosen that good part, which shall not be taken away from her. (Luke 10:41-42)

For Mary, sitting at the feet of the Master took priority over being the perfect host. She recognized that it was an extraordinary opportunity for King Jesus to visit their home and share His teachings and wisdom.

I believe that King Jesus agreed with Mary's decision because He knew that He had a greater purpose for His visit. On that day, it was more important for King Jesus *to serve rather than be served.* He came to serve Martha and Mary wisdom. He came to give them an eternal gift **that could not be taken away.** Martha almost missed the opportunity because she was distracted by hosting—something that she thought should take priority at that moment. Thankfully, the Lord encouraged Martha to readjust her priorities and take advantage of His presence.

Like Martha, we too can focus so much on the details and tasks of life that we miss moments when God wants to share His wisdom and revelation with us. It is important for us to evaluate if the demands of life, service, career, and ministry are causing us to miss out on spending time with the Lord. It is good for us to work hard and to serve, but sometimes the better choice is to stop and give the Lord our undivided attention. Like Mary, we may even have to disregard the priorities and responsibilities that others try to impose on us. Martha wanted Mary to focus on the meal, but Mary perceived that it was critical for her to sit and listen to what King Jesus wanted to present at that moment. He had prepared a feast for their souls!

BEING STILL AT THE MASTER'S FEET

Despite Martha's complaint, Mary remained still and undisturbed at the feet of King Jesus. His teaching captivated her attention. I can relate to Mary's determination to learn from the Master. It reminds me of the type of focus and concentration that I needed to have for the yearlong study of **Matthew 11:29.**

Can you imagine studying one passage of scripture for an entire year? For me to stay focused on that scripture, week after week, I had to listen intently to the voice of God. I had to commit to regular prayer, study, and meditation. Uncovering each layer of the Scripture demanded my patience, attentiveness, and an attitude of expectation. I needed the Lord to reveal the depths of **Matthew 11:29** and give me specific instructions on how to present the concept of **Learning from Him.**

One might think that preaching from the same scripture every week would have been monotonous and repetitive. On the contrary, it was a magnificent experience. I felt as though I were searching for gold in a riverbed: the more I searched, the more God revealed the precious metal of His Word. But that period of revelation would not have occurred if I had not set aside quality time to be still in the presence of God.

King Jesus Himself was an example of the importance of setting aside time with God for prayer and meditation. Many passages of Scripture highlight His commitment to communicating with His Father. In **Luke 6:12**, the author says, **"And it came to pass in those days, that he went out into a mountain to pray, and continued all night in prayer to God."**
The fellowship that King Jesus had with His Father is not like the time that some of us dedicate to God. Sometimes we can be in such a hurry and so anxious when we talk to Him, that even after five minutes, we begin to think that a significant amount of time has passed. However, the truth is that we have spent very little time with the Father at all.

We live in such a fast-paced society. We have faster and more convenient methods of transportation, communication, and commerce. And although our culture may thrive on convenience and speed for managing the affairs of life, for our spiritual lives, faster is not always better. When it comes to the matters of the soul, there are times when we need to slow down. Consider this: we can sit still for a two-hour movie, one-hour television program, and a 30-minute phone conversation. What if we were to display the same patience and attentiveness during our time of prayer and meditation?

It is essential that we set aside time to hear the Lord's voice. Going to church services and serving in ministries is wonderful, but there are times when we need to be still at the Lord's feet and allow Him to be our teacher.

It is worthwhile to reiterate that the Lord is always available to share His wisdom with us. He offers His Word to all who want *to learn from Him*. Mary sat at the feet of King Jesus; this was a sign of her humility before the Lord and her sincere desire to hear His words. We too can sit at the feet of King Jesus by humbling ourselves to study His Word, listen to His voice, and learn His ways.

I encourage you to spend quality time communicating with God and meditating on His Word. I assure you, He will speak to the specific needs of your life.

WHAT YOU CAN EXPECT TO LEARN ON THIS JOURNEY

Learning from King Jesus is a very broad concept. King Jesus' life and teachings encompass more than what we can grasp in a year or even in a lifetime. However, this book highlights key principles from King Jesus' life and teachings that will help us to manifest the power of the Kingdom of God in our lives.

On this journey of **learning from King Jesus**, you can expect to learn: your significance as a Kingdom Citizen; how to manifest your Kingdom potential; the importance of sharing the Kingdom message and principles with others; and how to live free of religious burdens. You will come to know the true source of your peace and prosperity, understand your relationship to God, and embrace your purpose as a Kingdom Citizen.

You will learn how to elevate your thinking and triumph over fear, insecurity, condemnation, and poverty. You will learn the power and privileges of being a Citizen of the Kingdom of God, the benefits of serving others, and the importance of having an impact on your world and future generations.

Learning from King Jesus will lead you to His wisdom—wisdom that will give you the keys to life in the Kingdom.

Note: Throughout the book I refer to Jesus as "King Jesus." My intention is for us to think of Jesus Christ as the King of Kings who represents God's Kingdom on Earth and continues to reign on Earth through Believers."

> *And he hath on his vesture and on his thigh a name written,* KING OF KINGS, AND OF LORDS. *(Revelation 19:16)*

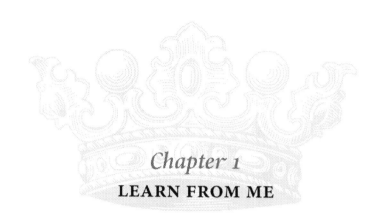

Chapter 1
LEARN FROM ME

Now that we understand that learning from King Jesus requires us to prioritize our time with Him, it is time to answer the essential question: What does it mean to **Learn from King Jesus?** When I reflect on this question, I instantly think of my son, Ruben William.

When my son was born, I knew there were many life skills and lessons that I would need to teach him. In addition to basic developmental skills, such as how to walk and talk, there were also spiritual insights that he would need to learn to be successful in life. For him to thrive, I would have to be his teacher and example. My son would have to learn from me. Just as earthly children rely on their parents for wisdom and guidance, Believers should look to King Jesus as our primary example and teacher to prevail in life and to fulfill His plans and purposes.

In this chapter, we will learn:

- To value the teachings of King Jesus
- To follow King Jesus by studying and applying His word
- To prioritize King Jesus' wisdom above human wisdom

THE CHALLENGE OF MAKING KING JESUS CHRIST
OUR #1 INFLUENCE

We live in a self-help culture. Bookstores carry thousands of titles dedicated to self-improvement. Motivational speakers and life coaches have become popular sources of guidance for people who want to change their lives. There are television programs that focus on weight loss, wealth-building, achieving personal goals, and improving our relationships. There are even churches and ministries that host national conferences dedicated to marriage, family, finance, and personal empowerment. People invest hundreds (and sometimes thousands) of dollars in discovering the keys to success, love, and happiness.

It is honorable to seek to become our best and to want to live quality lives. It is also prudent to seek out the advice and opinions of those who are experts in certain fields. But in our efforts to advance in life, we should look to the one who is the absolute authority on all matters of life. King Jesus' teachings should be our primary influence on issues pertaining to life and spirituality.

King Jesus came to Earth to present the central message of God's Kingdom: that a personal relationship with God and access to an abundant life in His Kingdom are available to all mankind:

> *17 From that time Jesus began to preach, and to say, Repent: for the kingdom of heaven is at hand. (Matthew 4:17)*

> *10 I am come that they might have life, and that they might have it more abundantly. (John 10:10b)*

During King Jesus' time of ministry, some people promoted a variety of religious practices and ideas that were contrary to God's Word. Although King Jesus found himself in an environment of competing philosophies, He remained steadfast in His proclamation of the arrival of the Kingdom and its promise of an abundant life. King Jesus' message of the Kingdom was new and thought-provoking. It stirred both curiosity and great controversy among those who heard it. Because King Jesus' message conflicted with some of the other teachings of that time, the religious leaders challenged His spiritual authority:

> *13 The Pharisees therefore said unto him, Thou bearest record of thyself; thy record is not true. (John 8:13)*

Despite opposition from religious leaders, thousands of people would gather to hear King Jesus teach. They were hungry to grasp the truth of God's Word, not just religious rhetoric.

King Jesus' teachings on the Kingdom are as powerful and relevant today as they were during His time on Earth. And even though society inundates us with modern views on life and spirituality, King Jesus' instruction, **"Learn from Me,"** beckons us to come to Him, give attention to His Word, and experience the power of the Kingdom of God.

Prioritizing the wisdom of Jesus Christ is something that all Believers will have to do in their spiritual journey. Even Jesus' disciples and apostles had to exchange religious traditionalism for the teachings of the Kingdom. The Apostle Paul was a religious zealot before he encountered the Kingdom of God. Once He learned the teachings of King Jesus and entered the Kingdom, He resolved to forsake ineffectual religious ideas and embrace the truth of God's Word:

> *7 But what things were gain to me, those I counted loss for Christ.*
> *8 Yea doubtless, and I count all things but loss for the excellency of the knowledge of Christ Jesus my Lord: for whom I have suffered the loss of all things, and do count them but dung, that I may win Christ.*
> *(Philippians 3:7-8)*

As I previously said, there are many well-educated and experienced theologians, ministers, psychologists, and spiritual leaders who claim to know the secrets of leading a meaningful life. And while their ideas may be reasonable, and even helpful, their knowledge and experience do not compare to the wisdom of King Jesus.

If you need convincing that King Jesus should be our primary authority on life, let's review His qualifications:

1. King Jesus Was Divinely Appointed to Be an Advocate for Humanity

God chose His Son to come to Earth to experience human challenges and to show men and women how to apply Kingdom principles to overcome those challenges. During His time on Earth, King Jesus gained deep compassion for the obstacles that humanity faced: the oppression of religion, the struggle against sin, and the pain of being separated from the presence of the Creator:

> *14 Seeing then that we have a great high priest, that is passed into the heavens, Jesus the Son of God, let us hold fast our profession.*

15 For we have not an high priest which cannot be touched with the feeling of our infirmities; but was in all points tempted like as we are, yet without sin.

16 Let us therefore come boldly unto the throne of grace, that we may obtain mercy, and find grace to help in time of need. (Hebrews 4:14-16)

2. King Jesus Was Divinely Appointed to Restore Man's Access to the Kingdom of God – Many people seek knowledge to lead successful and purposeful lives. What some of them do not understand is that the life they seek is in the Kingdom of God. Mankind was separated from the Kingdom when Adam, the first man, failed to obey God's instructions in the Garden of Eden (as recorded in **Genesis, Chapters 1-3**). God chose His Son to come to Earth to restore the relationship between God and man and to restore man's access to the Kingdom. Thus, King Jesus refers to Himself as **"the door"** to the Kingdom of God:

6 This parable spake Jesus unto them: but they understood not what things they were which he spake unto them.

7 Then said Jesus unto them again, Verily, verily, I say unto you, I am the door of the sheep.

8 All that ever came before me are thieves and robbers: but the sheep did not hear them.

9 I am the door: by me if any man enter in, he shall be saved, and shall go in and out, and find pasture. (John 10:6-9)

6 Jesus saith unto him, I am the way, the truth, and the life: no man cometh unto the Father, but by me. (John 14:6)

7 Who in the days of his flesh, when he had offered up prayers and supplications with strong crying and tears unto him that was able to save him from death, and was heard in that he feared;

8 Though he were a Son, yet learned he obedience by the things which he suffered;

9 And being made perfect, he became the author of eternal salvation unto all them that obey him. (Hebrews 5:7-9)

3. King Jesus Was Divinely Appointed to Proclaim and Teach the Ways of the Kingdom – God appointed King Jesus to proclaim the Kingdom's presence, power, and availability to all who would receive it. The Son of God was not only divinely qualified to teach the Kingdom's message but also the only being on Earth who could bear witness to the Kingdom's truth, power, and splendor. Who better to teach mankind Kingdom principles and culture than the King Himself—Jesus Christ:

> *34 While he thus spake, there came a cloud, and overshadowed them: and they feared as they entered into the cloud.*
> *35 And there came a voice out of the cloud, saying, This is my beloved Son: hear him. (Luke 9:34-35)*

> *12 I have spoken to you of earthly things and you do not believe; how then will you believe if I speak of heavenly things?*
> *13 No one has ever gone into heaven except the one who came from heaven—the Son of Man. (John 3:12-13 NIV)*

> *38 For I came down from heaven, not to do mine own will, but the will of him that sent me. (John 6:38)*

I presented evidence that King Jesus should be our authority on life not because His authority needs human validation, but because we often take His wisdom for granted. We place religion, the ideas of men, and our opinions above His truth. Fortunately, King Jesus' record speaks for itself. He invites us to **learn from Him** because He knows that He is the only one who can lead us to the eternal truths and answers that we seek. King Jesus has our best interest at heart. Let us commit to *learning from Him!*

WILLING TO FOLLOW

When I again reflect on my experience of raising my son, I notice a key principle that applies to our process of learning from King Jesus. As a child, my son had to trust my guidance for the sake of his protection and happiness. He essentially had to follow my lead.

The same is true for us. If we want to experience life in the Kingdom of God, we should trust King Jesus' wisdom and choose to follow His blueprint for living. King Jesus invites us to follow Him because He is the only one who can show us how to live life at an optimal level and experience the Kingdom here on Earth:

> *12 Then spake Jesus again unto them, saying, I am the light of the world: he that followeth me shall not walk in darkness, but shall have the light of life. (John 8:12)*

As I thought about King Jesus' invitation to follow and learn from Him, I realized that it could impose considerable pressure if not correctly understood. To learn from Him means to commit to living at a high level of character, maturity, and integrity. Initially, learning from King Jesus may seem intimidating, but the Lord promises that it is rewarding. In **Matthew 11:29**, the Lord says, **"[If you *learn from me*, you will find rest for your souls]."** Could there be a greater benefit than that?

The idea of learning from King Jesus' example should not be a burden to us; it should encourage and motivate us. King Jesus describes learning from Him as a **"yoke [that] is easy"** and **"a burden [that] is light"** (**Matthew 11:30 NIV**). He uses the terms "easy" and "light" because He sent the Holy Spirit to dwell within Believers to help us follow in His ways:

> *16 And I will pray the Father, and he will give you another Helper, that He may abide with you forever—*
> *17 The Spirit of truth, whom the world cannot receive, because it neither sees Him nor knows Him; but you know Him, for He dwells with you and will be in you. (John 14:16-17 New King James Version)*

Some people would rather live a life of moral flexibility than make an effort to develop and grow. Instead of anticipating the difficulty in following King Jesus, we should focus on the promise of peace and rest that comes when we choose to learn from Him. Do not be a person who says or thinks, *"I can't be like King Jesus. I am weak and limited."* Beware of making such a negative declaration; it is simply not true. As a Child of the King, you possess the seed of His Spirit—His nature and characteristics. You have the power and potential to be like King Jesus Christ and walk in His ways:

> *3 His divine power has given us everything we need for a godly life through our knowledge of him who called us by his own glory and goodness.*
> *4 Through these he has given us his very great and precious promises, so that through them you may participate in the divine nature, having escaped the corruption in the world caused by evil desires. (2 Peter 1:3-4 NIV)*

Sometimes we make matters of spiritual living more difficult than necessary because we hesitate to believe and follow King Jesus' instructions. Despite our resistance, King Jesus made our choice very clear. If we want to grow in spiritual understanding, He says, **"learn from Me."** It may seem challenging to grow in the ways of King Jesus, but it is possible if we are willing. Instead of questioning our ability to learn from and follow King Jesus, we should affirm to ourselves, *"I can be like Him!"*

A HUNGER FOR HIS WORD

To **learn from King Jesus**, not only must we follow Him, but we must also have a hunger for His Word. The Word of God provides spiritual nourishment that sustains and energizes the soul of every Believer:

> *4 But he answered and said, It is written, Man shall not live by bread alone, but by every word that proceedeth out of the mouth of God. (Matthew 4:4)*

A colleague of mine once told me the story of a young woman who loved to eat cake. No matter the occasion, she would always take her time eating her slice because she loved to savor each bite. Even as a child, it would take her much longer than the other children in her family to finish her dessert. While she would be enjoying her cake, her older brother would walk by and ask, "Are you still eating that?"

How often do we as Believers take the time to savor our experiences with the Lord? How often does our hunger for His Word lead us to set aside extra time to study and meditate on its truth? During our yearlong study of **Matthew 11:29**, the congregation of Centro Diplomático could have easily asked, "Are we still eating this?" Instead, we had the same attitude as the young woman: we wanted to savor all the wisdom of that Scripture.

I feel that some Believers are hesitant to study God's Word because they know it will challenge them to change thoughts and behaviors that are contrary to the Kingdom. But we should not be afraid of God's Word. As we **learn from King Jesus**, we should expect for His Word to inspire us to grow and mature. Not every word from God will be easy to accept, but it will always be for our good:

> *60 On hearing it, many of his disciples said, "This is a hard teaching. Who can accept it?"*
> *61 Aware that his disciples were grumbling about this, Jesus said to them, "Does this offend you?*
> *62 Then what if you see the Son of Man ascend to where he was before!*

63 The Spirit gives life; the flesh counts for nothing. The words I have spoken to you—they are full of the Spirit and life. (John 6:60-63 NIV)

12 For the word of God is quick, and powerful, and sharper than any twoedged sword, piercing even to the dividing asunder of soul and spirit, and of the joints and marrow, and is a discerner of the thoughts and intents of the heart. (Hebrews 4:12)

HEARING THE WORD WITH THE RIGHT HEART

Whenever we hear God's Word, it is an opportunity for us to improve our lives. It is very important for us to hear the Word with the right heart because that is the only way it will transform our lives. When a minister or teacher speaks the Word of God, he dispenses seeds of the Kingdom. When we hear the Word with the right heart, it means that we allow those seeds to penetrate our souls so we can apply what we have heard to our lives. King Jesus illustrated this in the "Parable of the Sower":

18 "Listen then to what the parable of the sower means:
19 When anyone hears the message about the kingdom and does not understand it, the evil one comes and snatches away what was sown in their heart. This is the seed sown along the path.
20 The seed falling on rocky ground refers to someone who hears the word and at once receives it with joy.
21 But since they have no root, they last only a short time. When trouble or persecution comes because of the word, they quickly fall away.
22 The seed falling among the thorns refers to someone who hears the word, but the worries of this life and the deceitfulness of wealth choke the word, making it unfruitful.
23 But the seed falling on good soil refers to someone who hears the word and understands it. This is the one who produces a crop, yielding a hundred, sixty or thirty times what was sown." (Matthew 13:18-23 NIV)

The Word of God will only change our lives if our hearts are good soil, meaning that we hear and receive the Word with faith and obedience. When we obey the Word's instructions, we enjoy the benefits of its harvest.

Furthermore, we should have the right attitude toward those ordained to teach God's Word. Sadly, I have noticed that some Believers are only willing to listen to the Word if, according to them, the *right* person is teaching. That is incorrect! We should be mature enough to listen to the

Word of God no matter the vessel that God chooses to use. Even a young child can stand in the pulpit and teach the Word if God has called him. We should focus on *the content of the message, not the container of the message.* Otherwise, we may miss a critical message for our lives:

> *13 For this reason we also thank God without ceasing, because when you received the word of God which you heard from us, you welcomed it not as the word of men, but as it is in truth, the word of God, which also effectively works in you who believe. (I Thessalonians 2:13 NKJV)*

Psalm 42:7 says, **"Deep calleth unto to deep."** The "deep" refers the soul of man and the Spirit of God. The deep also refers to the depth of our desire for God's presence and Word. When the soul of a man has a yearning for God's presence and Word, it cries out to God's Spirit. If your soul has a sincere desire for God's Word, then you will be stirred to open your heart the moment you hear it. You will be mature enough to look beyond the messenger to receive the message. Are you deep enough to listen and extract wisdom from the teachings regardless of the speaker? I encourage you to open your heart to God's Word no matter the style of the presenter.

SEEKING THE WORD OR SEEKING SIGNS AND MIRACLES

When I think of the remarkable experience I had studying **Matthew 11:29**, I can only imagine how phenomenal it must have been to listen to King Jesus teach during His time on Earth. King Jesus' teachings had a powerful effect on people. Whether He was teaching at the home of Mary and Martha or speaking to massive crowds in the desert, His words always held the attention of those who listened. King Jesus' words were so captivating that He once spoke to a crowd of four thousand people for three straight days:

> *1 In those days, the multitude being very great and having nothing to eat, Jesus called His disciples to Him and said to them,*
> *2 "I have compassion on the multitude, because they have now continued with Me three days and have nothing to eat.*
> *3 And if I send them away hungry to their own houses, they will faint on the way; for some of them have come from afar."*
> *4 Then His disciples answered Him, "How can one satisfy these people with bread here in the wilderness?"*
> *5 He asked them, "How many loaves do you have?"*

And they said, "Seven."
6 So He commanded the multitude to sit down on the ground. And He
took the seven loaves and gave thanks, broke them and gave them to His
disciples to set before them; and they set them before the multitude.
7 They also had a few small fish; and having blessed them, He said to set
them also before them.
8 So they ate and were filled, and they took up seven large baskets of
leftover fragments.
9 Now those who had eaten were about four thousand. And He sent
them away. (Mark 8:1-9 NKJV)

King Jesus not only spoke to the crowd for three days, but He also fed them by multiplying a few fish and loaves of bread. Usually, when we hear teachings on this passage, the emphasis is placed on the miracle of King Jesus multiplying the fish and bread. In my opinion, when we focus on the miracle, we neglect to see what is central to the story: just how captivating the teachings of King Jesus must have been for people to stay in a desert environment for three days without complaining.

Can you grasp the significance of this? Do you think that in our modern world masses of people would sit and listen to the most brilliant teacher for three days in a row without taking a break? No, I do not think so—not even in an air-conditioned room with food. But because of King Jesus' powerful ministry, four thousand people disregarded their comfort and stayed for three days because He spoke to the needs of their souls. They perceived the value of King Jesus' message and did not want to miss a word of His teachings.

The Bible has several accounts of crowds gathering to see King Jesus perform miracles. But in this case, the crowd wanted more. They wanted to listen to His Word. I found this fascinating! After pondering the crowd's motivation to listen to King Jesus for three days, the Spirit of the Lord asked me, *"Are you only impressed with Jesus' miracles? What about His words?"*

We should ask ourselves if we are following King Jesus for His miracles or His message. Are we following Him for the comforts and benefits that He can provide or do we have a sincere passion for learning His ways and Kingdom teachings? Just like the four thousand, we must be so determined to **learn from King Jesus** that we do not even place our desire to see signs and miracles above learning His ways.

A LIFETIME OF LEARNING

Have you ever watched a film based on someone's life? For the lead actor to present a convincing portrayal, he must be able to imitate the person's characteristics: their mannerisms, speech, and style of dress. The actor must also embody the individual's attitude and personality. It may take an actor months, and possibly years, of preparation to present an authentic representation.

The actor's preparation is much like our process of learning from King Jesus. Although the Bible does not instruct Believers to "pretend" to be King Jesus, it does encourage us to strive to be like Him in all our ways. The only way we can continue to grow into the image and likeness of King Jesus is to dedicate ourselves to studying and practicing His Word and ways:

> *24 Then said Jesus unto his disciples, If any man will come after me, let him deny himself, and take up his cross, and follow me.*
> *25 For whosoever will save his life shall lose it: and whosoever will lose his life for my sake shall find it. (Matthew 16:24-25)*

> *1 Be ye therefore followers of God, as dear children;*
> *2 And walk in love, as Christ also hath loved us, and hath given himself for us an offering and a sacrifice to God for a sweetsmelling savour. (Ephesians 5:1-2)*

> *9 Those things, which ye have both learned, and received, and heard, and seen in me, do: and the God of peace shall be with you. (Philippians 4:9)*

> *15 But as he which hath called you is holy, so be ye holy in all manner of conversation;*
> *16 Because it is written, Be ye holy; for I am holy. (I Peter 1:15-16)*

When I think of King Jesus' words, **"Learn from Me,"** I believe that it is a lifelong invitation. There is always a deeper level of His teachings for us to discover and apply to our lives.

KINGDOM REFLECTION

King Jesus is the Believer's blueprint and example for Kingdom living. Learning from Him means that we should look to Him as our authority on life, have a hunger for His word, cherish opportunities to listen to His voice, and make a lifelong commitment to following His ways. When we follow King Jesus' teachings, we can be confident that we are on the path of enlightenment. Our reflection of Christ and the Kingdom of God will shine brighter each day.

KINGDOM CHALLENGE

Do you long for a closer relationship with God? Do you need greater wisdom and guidance? Do you have a desire to be more like King Jesus and for your life to reflect the power and influence of the Kingdom of God? Decide and commit to prioritizing your time with the Lord. Designate a time each day to spend with Him in focused prayer, study, and meditation on His Word. Make a note of any revelations and instructions that the Lord gives you concerning your life. I guarantee that you will experience great joy as you sit at the Master's feet and take pleasure in the truth and wisdom of His words:

> *If any of you lacks wisdom, you should ask God, who gives generously to all without finding fault, and it will be given to you. (James 1:5 NIV)*

Chapter 2
LEARNING TO REST

Jesus promised that if we learn from Him, we will receive the ultimate gift of rest for our souls. To illustrate Jesus' concept of rest, I would like to use the example of taking a road trip. The most crucial tool for a driver to take on a long journey is a functioning GPS (Global Positioning System). For the Believer, the long trip is life, and the GPS is the Word of God.

In addition to having proper directions and guidance, one of the most important rules of being on the road is to know when to stop and rest. Along U.S. highways, there are signs posted at various rest areas. These stops allow drivers to refill their gas tank, stretch their legs, have something to eat, and go to sleep. Without stopping to rest, the driver could become fatigued and have difficulty concentrating; ignore directions and become lost; and in the worst-case scenario, endanger himself and others on the road.

Just like taking advantage of rest areas is necessary on a road trip, the human soul has a need for rest on the journey of life. The only way to obtain rest for the soul is to **learn from Jesus** and His Word:

> 28 *"Come to me, all you who are weary and burdened, and I will give you rest.*
> 29 *Take my yoke upon you and learn from me, for I am gentle and humble in heart, and you will find rest for your souls."*
> *(Matthew 11:28-29 NIV)*

What does it mean to obtain rest for the soul? When we think of rest, we may think it means physical repose or to take time out from the hectic pace of life; however, this is not what Jesus meant. Of course, the Lord wants us to rest our bodies, but in **Matthew 11:29**, Jesus' emphasis on rest has a deeper meaning. Those who **learn from Him** will find rest in the form of inner peace—a lasting sense of assurance and tranquility while here on Earth:

> *1 Therefore being justified by faith, we have peace with God through our Lord Jesus Christ:*
> *2 By whom also we have access by faith into this grace wherein we stand, and rejoice in hope of the glory of God. (Romans 5:1-2)*

In this chapter, we will learn:

- Jesus' concept of rest
- What it means to experience rest from religion
- Rest as the remedy for spiritual emptiness

REST FROM RELIGION

I believe one of the greatest challenges to experiencing inner rest is the burden of religion. Many Believers have become weary because they are preoccupied with religious rules and regulations that weigh them down and disturb their sense of peace with God. They long to have rest for their tired souls because they have only been exposed to religion and not the message of the Kingdom. (I will discuss the differences between religion and the Kingdom of God in Chapter 4, "Learning to Distinguish the Kingdom of God from Religion"). Many of them are seeking fulfillment, spiritual guidance, and purpose, but they have exhausted their souls (their emotional engines) with incorrect and religious teachings.

Those who need rest from religion tend to view the church as a gathering place made of bricks and pews and as a place that is under the jurisdiction of a certain denomination or religious association. They regularly attend Sunday services, but their souls continue to be empty and without peace. Their religious practices are oppressive instead of empowering. Some of these people are even under the religious control of leaders who use guilt and fear to bind people to their congregations.

There are also those who have no rest because they rely on religion to ease the guilt from mistakes they have made. They believe that the practice of certain rituals will appease their conscience and put them in good standing with God. However, religion can only provide temporary relief for the conscience. Only Jesus Christ can position the Believer in right standing with God and heal the guilt and regrets of the soul.

Many people in Jesus' time lacked inner peace because of the unnecessary rules placed upon them by religious leaders. They were not experiencing the true peace of being in a relationship with God. Instead, they were carrying the burdens of religious oppression, fear, condemnation, and weariness. Fortunately, Jesus came to offer them relief from these burdens. He came to offer them rest for their souls:

> 1 Then Jesus said to the crowds and to his disciples:
> 2 "The teachers of the law and the Pharisees sit in Moses' seat.
> 3 So you must be careful to do everything they tell you. But do not do what they do, for they do not practice what they preach.
> 4 They tie up heavy, cumbersome loads and put them on other people's shoulders, but they themselves are not willing to lift a finger to move them. (Matthew 23:1-4 NIV)

Entering the Kingdom of God gives rest from religion because it confirms the true source of our righteousness. It is not our behavior, ability to keep rules, or our deeds that make us righteous. Rather, it is our faith in Christ, who forgives our mistakes and covers our faults and imperfections with *His righteousness*, that makes us righteous in the eyes of God.

In the **Book of John**, Jesus met a woman at a well in the town of Samaria. While she was filling her vessels, He asked her for a drink of water. The woman was shocked that Jesus engaged her in conversation because Jews and Samaritans had very poor relations. Moreover, scholars suggest that the woman was surprised that Jesus spoke to her because she may have been considered an outcast in her community due to her unorthodox lifestyle. She had several previous marriages, and at the time that she met Jesus, she was living with a man who was not her husband. Remarkably, Jesus did not judge nor condemn the woman for her lifestyle. Instead, He confronted the real issue of her life: the emptiness of her soul:

> 13 Jesus answered, "Everyone who drinks this water will be thirsty again,
> 14 But whoever drinks the water I give them will never thirst. Indeed, the water I give them will become in them a spring of water welling up to eternal life."
> 15 The woman said to him, "Sir, give me this water so that I won't get thirsty and have to keep coming here to draw water."

16 He told her, "Go, call your husband and come back."
17 "I have no husband," she replied. Jesus said to her, "You are right when you say you have no husband.
18 The fact is, you have had five husbands, and the man you now have is not your husband. What you have just said is quite true."
19 "Sir," the woman said, "I can see that you are a prophet.
20 Our ancestors worshiped on this mountain, but you Jews claim that the place where we must worship is in Jerusalem."
21 "Woman," Jesus replied, "believe me, a time is coming when you will worship the Father neither on this mountain nor in Jerusalem.
22 You Samaritans worship what you do not know; we worship what we do know, for salvation is from the Jews.
23 Yet a time is coming and has now come when the true worshipers will worship the Father in the Spirit and in truth, for they are the kind of worshipers the Father seeks.
24 God is spirit, and his worshipers must worship in the Spirit and in truth." (John 4:13-24 NIV)

The woman at the well is a prime example of someone whose religion had failed her. Even though she was knowledgeable about her peoples' religious traditions, it was clear that her knowledge of those traditions had done little to help her. Jesus perceived that she was suffering from spiritual thirst instead of living a life of fulfillment:

13 Jesus answered, "Everyone who drinks this water will be thirsty again,
14 But whoever drinks the water I give them will never thirst. Indeed, the water I give them will become in them a spring of water welling up to eternal life." (John 4:13-14 NIV)

Just as water is critical for maintaining the body's health and existence, Jesus offered the woman spiritual water that would forever sustain and satisfy the needs of her life. Neither her knowledge of religion nor her relationships with men could fulfill her. Her sense of fulfillment could only come from a relationship with God. Because Jesus addressed the core issue of the woman's life, from that moment on, she would experience true contentment and lasting peace.

Just like the woman at the well, the same void of the soul persists for all who do not understand that engaging in religious practices will never lead us to the rest that Jesus can provide. Religion can only take away from our lives because it has no spiritual substance or power. It can only cause us to hunger and thirst for true peace, joy, and wisdom.

I can genuinely say that I obtained rest in my life when I understood that God never intended for man to practice religion. When we **learn from Jesus** and follow His teachings of the Kingdom of God, we can be free of the rules of men that cause us to feel guilty, oppressed, and thirsting for truth. He will instruct us on how to develop our souls and lead us to the only path of spiritual refreshment and satisfaction. There is no one better to guide us to the truth and rest than Jesus—the one who said, **"Learn from Me."**

SEARCH NO MORE

Like the woman at the well, many people today are suffering from emptiness in their souls. Not only do they turn to religion, but some also choose to fill the voids in their lives with all manner of addictions, unhealthy and abusive relationships, and desperate forms of pleasure-seeking. Countless people have even died from drug abuse and suicide because of their painful and fruitless search to discover a sense of peace and fulfillment.

Some people may attribute their feelings of emptiness to issues such as financial challenges, lack of purpose, loss of loved ones, romantic frustrations, and troubled relationships. But these issues are not the underlying cause of their emptiness. The root of their emptiness is a lack of connection to the Creator's love and His Kingdom:

1 "I am the true vine, and my Father is the gardener.
2 He cuts off every branch in me that bears no fruit, while every branch that does bear fruit he prunes so that it will be even more fruitful.
3 You are already clean because of the word I have spoken to you.
4 Remain in me, as I also remain in you. No branch can bear fruit by itself; it must remain in the vine. Neither can you bear fruit unless you remain in me.
5 "I am the vine; you are the branches. If you remain in me and I in you, you will bear much fruit; apart from me you can do nothing.
6 If you do not remain in me, you are like a branch that is thrown away and withers; such branches are picked up, thrown into the fire and burned.
7 If you remain in me and my words remain in you, ask whatever you wish, and it will be done for you.
8 This is to my Father's glory, that you bear much fruit, showing yourselves to be my disciples.

9 "As the Father has loved me, so have I loved you. Now remain in my love.

10 If you keep my commands, you will remain in my love, just as I have kept my Father's commands and remain in his love.

11 I have told you this so that my joy may be in you and that your joy may be complete. (John 15:1-11 NIV)

Humanity will continue a desperate (and even tragic) search to find the missing piece to the puzzle of life. It is only through obtaining salvation and entering the Kingdom of God that we can connect and deepen the relationship with our Creator. It is in that moment of connection that life can begin to make sense and that we can experience true fulfillment and peace.

Dear reader, if you feel burdened by tradition and religion, troubled by your circumstances, unenlightened about how to live a more meaningful life, and you want to have a real connection with our Creator, I encourage you to come to Christ and find rest. He offers you rest no matter who you are or what you have done. This rest assures that you have access to His wisdom; that you can be free from the demands, control, and constraints of religion; and that you are on a path of purpose, peace, and significance.

KINGDOM REFLECTION

If someone were to ask me what has been the most rewarding aspect of being a Believer, I would tell that person that my greatest reward has been finding rest for my soul. Some Believers speak of the personal achievements and spiritual advancements that they have made, but I will always emphasize how wonderful life has been because I have found rest by **learning from Jesus.** Jesus assures us that learning from Him is not a burden on the soul. Instead, we find peace and rest when we look to Jesus and His Word to structure and guide our lives.

Just like the woman at the well, our lives are transparent before the Lord. He can see the thirst within us. Religion, rituals, drugs, food and even people can never fulfill the voids and deep longings of our souls. Rather than judge us, Jesus shows us compassion by inviting us to quench our thirst by connecting with our Creator and partaking of His Word.

KINGDOM CHALLENGE

Do you have voids in your life that you have filled with unhealthy relationships or habits? I encourage you to go to the Lord in prayer. Do not fear condemnation from Him because of your challenges or the choices you have made. Tell Him the deepest longings of your soul. The Lord will teach you how to fill those empty places with the truth of His Word.

I encourage you to keep learning from Jesus!

> *Let us then approach God's throne of grace with confidence, so that we may receive mercy and find grace to help us in our time of need. (Hebrews 4:16 NIV)*

Chapter 3
LEARNING THE KINGDOM OF GOD

Learning from Jesus gives us the opportunity to understand the Kingdom that He came to proclaim. The Kingdom of God is His sovereign rule and influence in both Heaven and Earth. Jesus came to reveal the great mysteries of the Kingdom's principles, power, and benefits.

In this chapter, we will learn:

- How man lost and regained access to the Kingdom of God
- The power and function of the Kingdom
- The Believer's purpose and place in the Kingdom

A KINGDOM LOST AND FOUND

In the first two chapters of the book, I briefly focused on the restoration of man's access to the Kingdom of God. But to help us appreciate the significance of that restoration, I would like to discuss how man lost his access to the Kingdom.

I once heard the story of a creative young boy who built a toy boat out of wood. When the boy completed the boat, he knew that he had done a good job, so he was quite satisfied. One day, he decided to take the boat sailing. As it drifted along the river, a wave came and carried it away. The boy desperately ran alongside the river to rescue the boat, but he failed. It was as if the river had swallowed it up. The boy went home crying and very upset. He told his parents, "I lost the little boat that I loved in the river."

One day, the boy and his father went into town and happened to see the boat in a store window. The boy knew the boat was his because he had painted his name on it. He immediately went to the store owner to inquire about buying the boat, but the owner told him that it was not for sale. The boy refused to give up. He went back to the store and insisted so much on buying the boat that the owner finally sold it to him. The boy returned home very happy because he had recovered the boat that was now twice his own.

If we relate this story to the spiritual realm, we can say the following: God created man with His very own hands. One day, because of the waves of life (waves of pleasure, lies, disobedience, and wrong actions), mankind left God's protection and drifted down the river of separation into the realm of darkness. Although God was once able to claim man as His own, He now had to purchase man's soul from the kingdom of darkness. God sent Jesus to pay the price for that purchase through His death on a cross. Because of Jesus' sacrifice, humanity is now twice God's own: first because He created us and second because He purchased us from the powers of darkness and rescued us from the threat of eternal separation:

> *19 What? know ye not that your body is the temple of the Holy Ghost which is in you, which ye have of God, and ye are not your own?*
> *20 For ye are bought with a price: therefore glorify God in your body, and in your spirit, which are God's. (I Corinthians 6:19-20)*

> *13 When you were dead in your sins and in the uncircumcision of your flesh, God made you alive with Christ. He forgave us all our sins,*
> *14 Having canceled the charge of our legal indebtedness, which stood against us and condemned us; he has taken it away, nailing it to the cross. (Colossians 2:13-14 NIV)*

When God created Adam, he was without sin. Adam remained sinless until he failed to believe and obey God by observing the instructions that the Lord gave him in the Garden of Eden. Adam's unbelief and disobedience severed the relationship between God and man:

> *15 And the Lord God took the man, and put him into the garden of Eden to dress it and to keep it.*
> *16 And the Lord God commanded the man, saying, Of every tree of the garden thou mayest freely eat:*

17 But of the tree of the knowledge of good and evil, thou shalt not eat of it: for in the day that thou eatest thereof thou shalt surely die. (Genesis 2:15-17)

9 And the Lord God called unto Adam, and said unto him, Where art thou?
10 And he said, I heard thy voice in the garden, and I was afraid, because I was naked; and I hid myself (Genesis 3:9-10).

15 And I will put enmity between thee and the woman, and between thy seed and her seed; it shall bruise thy head, and thou shalt bruise his heel. (Genesis 3:15)

23 Therefore the Lord God sent him forth from the garden of Eden, to till the ground from whence he was taken.
24 So he drove out the man; and he placed at the east of the garden of Eden Cherubims, and a flaming sword which turned every way, to keep the way of the tree of life. (Genesis 3:23-24)

Although the decision of Adam (later referred to in the New Testament as the "First Adam") caused a rift between God and all mankind, I am so grateful that God had a plan to repair the rift and redeem man back from darkness. God sent the "last" and sinless Adam (the Son of God) to restore God's relationship with man and to restore man's original place in God's Kingdom:

18 And all things are of God, who hath reconciled us to himself by Jesus Christ, and hath given to us the ministry of reconciliation;
19 To wit, that God was in Christ, reconciling the world unto himself, not imputing their trespasses unto them; and hath committed unto us the word of reconciliation. (2 Corinthians 5:18-19)

Jesus made man's restoration and redemption possible through His death on the cross and resurrection from the grave. Jesus' death served as payment for our mistakes, and His resurrection guarantees that after the death of our physical bodies, our souls will experience eternal life in God's presence:

4 That he was buried, that he was raised on the third day according to the Scriptures,
5 And that he appeared to Cephas, and then to the Twelve.

6 After that, he appeared to more than five hundred of the brothers and sisters at the same time. (I Corinthians 15:4-6a NIV)

4 But when the fullness of the time was come, God sent forth his Son, made of a woman, made under the law,
5 To redeem them that were under the law, that we might receive the adoption of sons.
6 And because ye are sons, God hath sent forth the Spirit of his Son into your hearts, crying, Abba, Father. (Galatians 4:4-6)

24 "He himself bore our sins" in his body on the cross, so that we might die to sins and live for righteousness; "by his wounds you have been healed." (I Peter 2:24 NIV)

We can return to God and His Kingdom by turning from our ways and accepting Jesus' gift of salvation. Salvation through Jesus (The Door to the Kingdom) allows us to reconnect to the spiritual realm—the realm of the Kingdom. When we accept Jesus' salvation, we experience a *spiritual rebirth*. It is at the moment of rebirth that we enter the Kingdom and family of God (**John 3:1-13**). We once again become His heirs and Citizens of His Kingdom.

THE GOOD NEWS OF THE KINGDOM

Jesus came to announce the re-establishment of His Kingdom on Earth, to demonstrate its power, to teach its principles, and to offer its privileges to all who would enter and believe. He also came to prepare those who would follow Him and carry out God's original intent for man's existence: to colonize the Earth with the Kingdom's culture and principles.

Dr. Myles Munroe, who did extensive research and writings on the Kingdom of God, shared the following in his book, *Rediscovering the Kingdom*:

> *Whatever area over which the authority of a government rests becomes that government's property. All of the authority, rights, and powers of the nation represented by that government are in effect on that property. In the same way, we are ambassadors of Christ and of the Kingdom of God. Our home, office, church, and, indeed, anywhere our influence extends becomes an "embassy" of Heaven.*[1]

Believers and Kingdom Citizens have a responsibility to expand the Kingdom by sharing its message and demonstrating its power:

> 20 We are therefore Christ's ambassadors, as though God were making his appeal through us. We implore you on Christ's behalf: Be reconciled to God. (2 Corinthians 5:20 NIV)

When we embrace our roles as Kingdom representatives, we show our commitment to **learning from Jesus** and continuing the work that mattered to Him—expanding the Kingdom on Earth:

> 35 And Jesus went about all the cities and villages, teaching in their synagogues, and preaching the gospel of the kingdom, and healing every sickness and every disease among the people.
> 36 But when he saw the multitudes, he was moved with compassion on them, because they fainted, and were scattered abroad, as sheep having no shepherd.
> 37 Then saith he unto his disciples, The harvest truly is plenteous, but the labourers are few;
> 38 Pray ye therefore the Lord of the harvest, that he will send forth labourers into his harvest. (Matthew 9:35-38)

Many people in the world feel lost and need the Kingdom message. As Citizens, we can expand the Kingdom by sharing the good news of its conquest, transformation, power, provisions, and benefits.

1. The Conquest of the Kingdom - The conquest of the Kingdom refers to Jesus restoring the spiritual position, power, and privileges that man lost in the Garden of Eden. God chose Jesus to re-establish His relationship with mankind, dominion on Earth, and access to true prosperity (finding one's identity and value in God and experiencing integral well-being). The conquest occurred through Jesus' death, burial, and resurrection. Through His sacrifice, Jesus waged a spiritual war against the powers of death and sin: **"And having disarmed the powers and authorities, he made a public spectacle of them, triumphing over them by the cross." (Colossians 2:15 NIV)**

By believing in Jesus' sacrifice and resurrection, and confessing Him as Savior, man would have the opportunity to experience change and restoration. Those who seek a connection to a higher power, supreme being, or divinity can find hope that the true and living God exists, that He wants to have a relationship with them, and that He welcomes them to share in His Kingdom.

2. The Transformation of the Kingdom - The transformation of the Kingdom refers to the power Believers receive to live by God's standards and principles. Transformation also refers to our potential to become a complete reflection of God and His Kingdom:

> *8 But now ye also put off all these; anger, wrath, malice, blasphemy, filthy communication out of your mouth.*
> *9 Lie not one to another, seeing that ye have put off the old man with his deeds;*
> *10 And have put on the new man, which is renewed in knowledge after the image of him that created him. (Colossians 3:8-10)*

The transformation process begins when we receive salvation, and our souls are instantly made new:

> *17 Therefore if any man be in Christ, he is a new creature: old things are passed away; behold, all things are become new. (2 Corinthians 5:17)*

And while our spirits are reborn at the moment of salvation, our minds require a different process of transformation. The mind is where we process emotions, thoughts, and perceptions and make decisions. We must renew our minds to reflect the transformation that has occurred in our souls. Paul emphasized the importance of this process in **Romans 12:1-2**:

> *1 I beseech you therefore, brethren, by the mercies of God, that ye present your bodies a living sacrifice, holy, acceptable unto God, which is your reasonable service.*
> *2 And be not conformed to this world: but be ye transformed by the renewing of your mind, that ye may prove what is that good, and acceptable, and perfect, will of God.*

Renewal of our minds becomes possible when we commit to learning from Jesus and putting His Word into practice. I will discuss the transformation of the mind in more detail in Chapter 7, "Learning to Elevate Our Thinking."

3. The Power of the Kingdom - Possessing Kingdom power means that Believers have the strength to overcome the challenges of life. In

Rediscovering the Kingdom, Dr. Munroe describes the essence of Kingdom power in the following manner:

> *Gone are the days of trying to overcome without going through. In spite of the affliction and opposition of the world we have learned to overpower the enemy by the power of the One who lives in us.*
>
> *The Kingdom of which we are a part is so powerful that we need not fear any potential opposition. Kingdom men and women say, "Bring on the problems," and we will advance right through them.*[2]

God promises that because He dwells within us, we have the power to live victoriously:

> [35] *Who shall separate us from the love of Christ? shall tribulation, or distress, or persecution, or famine, or nakedness, or peril, or sword?*
> [36] *As it is written, For thy sake we are killed all the day long; we are accounted as sheep for the slaughter.*
> [37] *Nay, in all these things we are more than conquerors through him that loved us. (Romans 8:35-37)*

4. The Provisions of the Kingdom – Because Earth is a colony of Heaven, the Citizens who live in the colony have the guaranteed support of Heaven's resources. In *Rediscovering the Kingdom*, Dr. Munroe illustrates the Kingdom's organizational makeup, distinct characteristics, and operations to support its Citizens in the following way:

> *All kingdoms are comprised of a number of components necessary for them to function effectively. All kingdoms, including the Kingdom of God, have:*

> - *A Health program – Healing;*
> - *An Education program – Teaching ministry of the Holy Spirit;*
> - *A Taxation system – Tithing;*
> - *A Central Communication system – Gifts of the Spirit;*
> - *A Diplomatic Corps – Ambassadors of Christ;*
> - *A System of Administration – the Ministration of the Spirit through mankind called the Church; and*
> - *An Economy – a system of Giving and Receiving (seed time and harvest time).*[3]

The provisions of God's Kingdom are all-encompassing and can meet every need of its Citizens. Kingdom provisions support our well-being as well as our efforts to expand the Kingdom of God on Earth:

> 24 "No one can serve two masters. Either you will hate the one and love the other, or you will be devoted to the one and despise the other. You cannot serve both God and money.
> 25 "Therefore I tell you, do not worry about your life, what you will eat or drink; or about your body, what you will wear. Is not life more than food, and the body more than clothes?
> 26 Look at the birds of the air; they do not sow or reap or store away in barns, and yet your heavenly Father feeds them. Are you not much more valuable than they?
> 27 Can any one of you by worrying add a single hour to your life?
> 28 "And why do you worry about clothes? See how the flowers of the field grow. They do not labor or spin.
> 29 Yet I tell you that not even Solomon in all his splendor was dressed like one of these.
> 30 If that is how God clothes the grass of the field, which is here today and tomorrow is thrown into the fire, will he not much more clothe you—you of little faith?
> 31 So do not worry, saying, 'What shall we eat?' or 'What shall we drink?' or 'What shall we wear?'
> 32 For the pagans run after all these things, and your heavenly Father knows that you need them.
> 33 But seek first his kingdom and his righteousness, and all these things will be given to you as well.
> 34 Therefore do not worry about tomorrow, for tomorrow will worry about itself. Each day has enough trouble of its own.
> (Matthew 6:24-34 NIV)

5. Success and Happiness in the Kingdom - God designed man to thrive. He wants His children to live with purpose and enjoy life, family, and the beauty of His creation. The Scripture tells us, "**[God] gives us richly all things to enjoy**" (I Timothy 6:17 NKJV). We can only experience true success and happiness when we have the presence of God in our lives. Our connection to Him leads us on a path of wisdom, peace, personal achievement, and abundance.

After the death of Moses, God appointed Joshua to lead the people of Israel. God wanted His people to experience a life filled with His presence and for them to be triumphant in their pursuit of the Promised Land. God spoke to Joshua and gave him a formula for the success of His people. We can learn from Joshua and the Israelite's experience of success:

> 5 No one will be able to stand against you all the days of your life. As I was with Moses, so I will be with you; I will never leave you nor forsake you.
> 6 Be strong and courageous, because you will lead these people to inherit the land I swore to their ancestors to give them.
> 7 "Be strong and very courageous. Be careful to obey all the law my servant Moses gave you; do not turn from it to the right or to the left, that you may be successful wherever you go.
> 8 Keep this Book of the Law always on your lips; meditate on it day and night, so that you may be careful to do everything written in it. Then you will be prosperous and successful.
> 9 Have I not commanded you? Be strong and courageous. Do not be afraid; do not be discouraged, for the Lord your God will be with you wherever you go." (Joshua 1:5-9 NIV)

When we **learn from Jesus'** ministry on Earth and His Word, He reveals the blessings, power, and transformation that are available to all who choose to experience life in God's Kingdom.

IDENTITY AND PURPOSE IN THE KINGDOM

When we reconnect to the King, we become His sons and daughters and receive the rights and benefits granted to all Kingdom heirs; this includes the opportunity to reign with Him:

> 11 He came unto his own, and his own received him not.
> 12 But as many as received him, to them gave the power to become the sons of God, even to them that believe on his name:
> 13 Which were born, not of blood, nor of the will of the flesh, nor of the will of man, but of God. (John 1:11-13)

The Believer's ability to reign and triumph in life, to fulfill his role as a Kingdom representative, and to share the Kingdom message with others is rooted in his confidence in and understanding of his Kingdom identity and purpose.

Many people in the world have no sense of purpose or direction in life. They have daily routines and responsibilities, but they have not discovered why they exist. Some have even had humble, and sometimes tragic, beginnings. They have experienced abuse and degradation at the hands of others and no longer have a sense of value or significance. I am thankful that despite the conditions of our past or present lives, God gives us a new identity and a unique purpose when we become Citizens of His Kingdom.

The life purpose of each Kingdom Citizen should first and foremost coincide with the agenda of the King: to expand the Kingdom of God on Earth. The King has blessed each of us with gifts, talents, and abilities that can help us carry out His will. When we understand God's plan for our lives, we can gain confidence in the value of our gifts to the Kingdom, and we can increase our impact on the world.

If we ever feel insecure about who we are or our purpose in the Kingdom, we can always look to Jesus' example to overcome those insecurities. He was sure of His identity as the Son of God and confident in His purpose to restore man back to the Kingdom of God:

> *21 Now when all the people were baptized, it came to pass, that Jesus also being baptized, and praying, the heaven was opened,*
> *22 And the Holy Ghost descended in a bodily shape like a dove upon him, and a voice came from heaven, which said, Thou art my beloved Son; in thee I am well pleased. (Luke 3:21-22)*

> *17 and the scroll of the prophet Isaiah was handed to him. Unrolling it, he found the place where it is written:*
> *18 "The Spirit of the Lord is on me, because he has anointed me to proclaim good news to the poor. He has sent me to proclaim freedom for the prisoners and recovery of sight for the blind, to set the oppressed free,*
> *19 To proclaim the year of the Lord's favor."*
> *20 Then he rolled up the scroll, gave it back to the attendant and sat down. The eyes of everyone in the synagogue were fastened on him.*
> *21 He began by saying to them, "Today this scripture is fulfilled in your hearing." (Luke 4:17-21 NIV)*

Even when people mocked Jesus, He never doubted His significance to the Kingdom and humanity:

> *23 And he said unto them, Ye will surely say unto me this proverb, Physician, heal thyself: whatsoever we have heard done in Capernaum, do also here in thy country.*

24 And he said, Verily I say unto you, No prophet is accepted in his own country. (Luke 4:23-24)

Like Jesus, we can be confident that when we enter the Kingdom, God restores our positions of spiritual significance, purpose, and power. In the **Book of Revelation**, the Apostle John referred to Believers as Kings and Priests saying, **"And hast made us unto our God kings and priests: and we shall reign on earth" (Revelation 5:10).**

Dr. Myles Munroe discusses the identity of Kingdom Citizens in *Rediscovering the Kingdom*:

> *[The] most outstanding element distinguishing the Kingdom of God from every other kingdom is the concept that all of its citizens are relatives of the King, and are kings themselves. This was the message brought to Earth by the Lord Jesus Christ.[4]*

The roles of kings and priests signify our ability to use our gifts effectively and to exercise our dominion on Earth:

> *26 And God said, Let us make man in our image, after our likeness: and let them have dominion over the fish of the sea, and over the fowl of the air, and over the cattle, and over all the earth, and over every creeping thing that creepeth upon the earth.*
> *27 So God created man in his own image, in the image of God created he him; male and female created he them.*
> *28 And God blessed them, and God said unto them, Be fruitful, and multiply, and replenish the earth, and subdue it: and have dominion over the fish of the sea, and over the fowl of the air, and over every living thing that moveth upon the earth. (Genesis 1:26-28)*

Kings are individuals who reign in their calling and take authority over their lives by exercising the "free will" that God has given every human being. Kings use their gifts to take the Kingdom message to the world. They influence humanity with Kingdom knowledge, principles, and impactful deeds. As Kings, we can use our gifts and talents to be industrious and productive leaders in the world. Whether our gifts are in business, government, medicine, technology, or the arts, God can use it to bring others into the Kingdom.

Priests have a calling to teach God's Word and manage ministry affairs. All Believers are equipped to share the Word, but He has called specific individuals to serve as Priests (pastors or ministers) to oversee the administration and functioning of the church, share the teachings of Jesus with their respective congregations, and appoint spiritual leaders. Those who serve as Priests can also be active leaders in their communities.

At Centro Diplomático, we emphasize the necessity of Kings and Priests. We encourage our congregation to serve in ministry and the community and to develop trustworthy businesses.

No matter our function (king, priest, or both), we all can help to expand the Kingdom of God on Earth and fulfill Jesus' mission to share its good news with others:

> *1 In my former book, Theophilus, I wrote about all that Jesus began to do and to teach*
> *2 Until the day he was taken up to heaven, after giving instructions through the Holy Spirit to the apostles he had chosen.*
> *3 After his suffering, he presented himself to them and gave many convincing proofs that he was alive. He appeared to them over a period of forty days and spoke about the kingdom of God.*
> *4 On one occasion, while he was eating with them, he gave them this command: "Do not leave Jerusalem, but wait for the gift my Father promised, which you have heard me speak about.*
> *5 For John baptized with water, but in a few days you will be baptized with the Holy Spirit."*
> *6 Then they gathered around him and asked him, "Lord, are you at this time going to restore the kingdom to Israel?"*
> *7 He said to them: "It is not for you to know the times or dates the Father has set by his own authority.*
> *8 But you will receive power when the Holy Spirit comes on you; and you will be my witnesses in Jerusalem, and in all Judea and Samaria, and to the ends of the earth." (Acts 1:1-8 NIV)*

KINGDOM REFLECTION

Jesus came to restore man's dominion on Earth and access to the Kingdom of God. Those who enter the Kingdom receive new identities as Sons and Daughters of God and Citizens of His Kingdom. Their past no longer defines them. They become new creatures and gain a divine calling to operate in the Earth as Kings and Priests, to share the Kingdom message and principles, and to use their gifts and talents to help improve the world (one individual at a time).

17 Therefore, if anyone is in Christ, the new creation has come: The old has gone, the new is here! (2 Corinthians 5:17 NIV)

9 But you are a chosen people, a royal priesthood, a holy nation, God's special possession, that you may declare the praises of him who called you out of darkness into his wonderful light. (I Peter 2:9 NIV)

KINGDOM CHALLENGE

Our culture is fascinated with the concept of the makeover. There are many television shows dedicated to individuals seeking to undergo a positive transformation, whether physical, emotional, or financial. As you continue this journey of **learning from Jesus** and applying His teachings, you will experience a spiritual makeover that will reflect in your character and your life. When people notice your progress, I encourage you to use it as an opportunity to share with them the transformative power of **learning from Jesus** and living as a Citizen of the Kingdom.

Please note: This chapter presented a basic introduction and overview of the Kingdom of God. The Kingdom is such a vast subject and demands in-depth study. To expand your knowledge of the Kingdom, I encourage you to continue to consult the Word of God. You may also supplement your study of the Word with reputable teachings. I highly recommend any materials written by Dr. Myles Munroe.

Chapter 4
LEARNING TO DISTINGUISH THE KINGDOM OF GOD FROM RELIGION

Learning from Jesus will enable us to distinguish between the Kingdom of God and religion. This knowledge is critical because it will transform how we see our relationship with God and our place in His Kingdom.

In this chapter, we will learn:

- How religion became part of the human experience (based only on Biblical accounts)
- The difference between Kingdom precepts and religious laws and rituals
- Why Jesus spoke so strongly against religious legalism and so passionately about the Kingdom

LIFE WITH THE CREATOR BEFORE RELIGION

In the Garden of Eden, Adam and Eve enjoyed a ritual-free, intimate relationship with God. They communed with Him freely; there was no need for religion or a spiritual mediator between them and God. They had no worries about their livelihood because they lived in a home that God had created just for them. He provided for their needs through the food the Garden produced, and He gave them dominion over the Earth and its creatures. God essentially blessed them with a perfect life:

> *26 And God said, Let us make man in our image, after our likeness: and let them have dominion over the fish of the sea, and over the fowl of the*

air, and over the cattle, and over all the earth, and over every creeping thing that creepeth upon the earth.

...

29 And God said, Behold, I have given you every herb bearing seed, which is upon the face of all the earth, and every tree, in the which is the fruit of a tree yielding seed; to you it shall be for meat. (Genesis 1:26, 29)

Unfortunately, the moment Adam and Eve chose to follow the serpent's suggestion to eat from the *Tree of the Knowledge of Good and Evil*, they abdicated their place of dominion over the Earth. Furthermore, because they did not trust God's Word and obey His command, Adam and Eve damaged their peaceful relationship with God and lost access to the Garden:

17 To Adam he said, "Because you listened to your wife and ate fruit from the tree about which I commanded you, 'You must not eat from it.' (Genesis 3:17 NIV)

23 So the Lord God banished him from the Garden of Eden to work the ground from which he had been taken.
24 After he drove the man out, he placed on the east side of the Garden of Eden cherubim and a flaming sword flashing back and forth to guard the way to the tree of life. (Genesis 3:23-24 NIV)

From the moment that Adam and Eve acted in unbelief and disobedience, humanity has struggled to recover its power (dominion) on Earth and relationship with God. Religion has been man's solution to recover what Adam lost in the Garden. Dr. Munroe expounds on man's need for religion in *Rediscovering the Kingdom*:

The human spirit longs for a world he can control where circumstances are at the mercy of his will. This is the greatest human desire. This is also the source and motivation of religious and spiritual development and practice.[1]

Although Adam's actions in the Garden resulted in the establishment of countless religions and beliefs, when we **learn from Jesus**, we come to understand that God presides over a Kingdom, not a religion:

17 From that time Jesus began to preach, and to say, Repent: for the kingdom of heaven is at hand. (Matthew 4:17)

EARLY EXAMPLES OF RELIGION IN THE BIBLE

After Adam and Eve's dismissal from the Garden of Eden and fall from the Kingdom, humanity developed and engaged in rituals to reconnect to the Creator. Below is a list of examples from the Bible of man's practice of religion (as we understand religious systems today):

1. Cain and Abel - Cain and Abel, sons of Adam and Eve, had an opportunity to worship God by presenting Him a gift. Abel was a shepherd, so he presented God with a sacrifice from his flock of sheep. Cain was a farmer and chose to present produce from his harvest. God accepted Abel's sacrifice, but He was not pleased with Cain's:

> *1 Adam made love to his wife Eve, and she became pregnant and gave birth to Cain. She said, "With the help of the Lord I have brought forth a man."*
>
> *2 Later she gave birth to his brother Abel. Now Abel kept flocks, and Cain worked the soil.*
>
> *3 In the course of time Cain brought some of the fruits of the soil as an offering to the Lord.*
>
> *4 And Abel also brought an offering—fat portions from some of the first-born of his flock. The Lord looked with favor on Abel and his offering,*
>
> *5 But on Cain and his offering he did not look with favor. So Cain was very angry, and his face was downcast.*
>
> *6 Then the Lord said to Cain, "Why are you angry? Why is your face downcast?*
>
> *7 If you do what is right, will you not be accepted? But if you do not do what is right, sin is crouching at your door; it desires to have you, but you must rule over it." (Genesis 4:1-7 NIV)*

Genesis is not specific about why God rejected Cain's offering, but in **Hebrews 11:4**, we do find more insight as to why God found favor with Abel's gift:

> *4 By faith Abel brought God a better offering than Cain did. By faith he was commended as righteous, when God spoke well of his offerings. And by faith Abel still speaks, even though he is dead. (NIV)*

The Lord was pleased with Abel's gift because Abel presented it with a heart of faith. Furthermore, some scholars suggest that Abel's sacrifice from his flock foreshadowed Jesus' act of redeeming man through His death on the cross. Jesus is often referred to in Scripture as the "Lamb of God," the one who would sacrifice himself for mankind:

> 29 *The next day John seeth Jesus coming unto him, and saith, Behold the Lamb of God, which taketh away the sin of the world. (John 1:29)*

Because the Scripture refers to Abel's gift as an act of faith, perhaps we can assume that God was displeased with Cain because he did not present his gift in a spirit of faith (**Hebrews 11:4**). Although Scripture does not mention the actual reason why God was displeased, I would like to suggest that Cain's offering was equivalent to a religious act because it did not meet God's standards. Cain presented his act of worship in a manner that God did not find acceptable. His story illustrates the failure of religion. Religion does not consider what God desires; it seeks to please God on man's terms. Cain's attempt to find favor with God disappointed God and left Cain envious of the approval that God bestowed on Abel.

Sadly, Cain reacted vengefully to God's displeasure by murdering Abel:

> 8 *Now Cain said to his brother Abel, "Let's go out to the field." While they were in the field, Cain attacked his brother Abel and killed him.*
> 9 *Then the Lord said to Cain, "Where is your brother Abel?" "I don't know," he replied. "Am I my brother's keeper?"*
> 10 *The Lord said, "What have you done? Listen! Your brother's blood cries out to me from the ground. (Genesis 4:8-10 NIV)*

In my opinion, Cain murdered Abel out of anger, envy, and spiritual frustration. We can compare Cain's behavior to the way religious people have behaved throughout history. People have waged devastating wars to preserve their religious ideas, to impose their religious beliefs on others, and to prove that they alone know the path to God. These types of wars and disputes reveal the danger of religion. It can leave a person empty of spiritual fulfillment, mislead a person in his pursuit of God, and have devastating effects on an individual and those around them.

2. The Tower of Babel - Before we examine how the Tower of Babel serves as an example of religion, we will first review the events that led to the Tower's construction—the most significant being the Great Flood.

In the **Book of Genesis**, the Earth suffered a flood due to man's disobedience and corruption:

> *11 Now the earth was corrupt in God's sight and was full of violence.*
> *12 God saw how corrupt the earth had become, for all the people on earth had corrupted their ways.*
> *13 So God said to Noah, "I am going to put an end to all people, for the earth is filled with violence because of them. I am surely going to destroy both them and the earth.*
> *14 So make yourself an ark of cypress wood; make rooms in it and coat it with pitch inside and out.*
>
> *17 I am going to bring floodwaters on the earth to destroy all life under the heavens, every creature that has the breath of life in it. Everything on earth will perish.*
> *18 But I will establish my covenant with you, and you will enter the ark—you and your sons and your wife and your sons' wives with you.*
> *(Genesis 6:11-14, 17-18 NIV)*

After the flood waters had subsided, men repopulated the Earth. As people settled and established cities, they decided that inhabiting the land was not enough. They wanted to expand their territory and power by building a tower that reached the heavens. They did not construct the tower to honor God; instead, they built it as a monument to their ingenuity. **Genesis 11:4** reads:

> *4 Then they said, "Come, let us build ourselves a city, with a tower that reaches to the heavens, so that we may make a name for ourselves; otherwise we will be scattered over the face of the whole earth." (NIV)*

Although the Bible does not refer to the Tower of Babel as a symbol of religion, the Tower's construction does expand our definition of religion to include the practice of idolatry. The decision to build the Tower was a sign that man had become a god unto himself. Rather than use their intelligence and talents to reverence God, the people chose to build the tower to honor themselves.

3. **Abraham** - The story of Abraham is unique from the previous examples. Abraham's is a story of someone who was called by God *to leave* his religious traditions.

In Joshua 24:2-4, we read:

2 Joshua said to all the people, "This is what the Lord, the God of Israel, says: 'Long ago your ancestors, including Terah the father of Abraham and Nahor, lived beyond the Euphrates River and worshiped other gods. 3 But I took your father Abraham from the land beyond the Euphrates and led him throughout Canaan and gave him many descendants. I gave him Isaac,
4 And to Isaac I gave Jacob and Esau. I assigned the hill country of Seir to Esau, but Jacob and his family went down to Egypt.'" (NIV)

God called Abraham from a tradition of idolatry into a relationship with Him. Abraham chose to follow in the ways of the Lord and to discover the promises that God had for him:

1 The Lord had said to Abram, "Go from your country, your people and your father's household to the land I will show you."
(Genesis 12:1 NIV)

56 Your father Abraham rejoiced to see my day: and he saw it, and was glad.
57 Then said the Jews unto him, Thou art not yet fifty years old, and hast thou seen Abraham?
58 Jesus said unto them, Verily, verily, I say unto you, Before Abraham was, I am.
59 Then took they up stones to cast at him: but Jesus hid himself, and went out of the temple, going through the midst of them, and so passed by. (John 8:56-59)

Because of Abraham's decision to follow God, all Believers are heirs of the blessings and promises that God made to Abraham. But we can only enjoy these promises by entering the Kingdom, not by practicing religion:

25 Ye are the children of the prophets, and of the covenant which God made with our fathers, saying unto Abraham, And in thy seed shall all the kindreds of the earth be blessed (Acts 3:25).

16 Therefore it is of faith, that it might be by grace; to the end the promise might be sure to all the seed; not to that only which is of the law, but to that also which is of the faith of Abraham; who is the father of us all. (Romans 4:16)

7 Understand, then, that those who have faith are children of Abraham.
8 Scripture foresaw that God would justify the Gentiles by faith, and an-
nounced the gospel in advance to Abraham: "All nations will be blessed
through you."
9 So those who rely on faith are blessed along with Abraham, the man of
faith. (Galatians 3:7-9 NIV)

29 And if ye be Christ's, then are ye Abraham's seed, and heirs according
to the promise. (Galatians 3:29)

THE KINGDOM OF GOD IS NOT A RELIGION

I express the following opinion carefully and sincerely: I believe that all religions (past and present) are the same. They seek to enlighten others on spiritual matters and the ways of God, they seek to define the meaning of life, they attempt to explain the origin of man, they claim to possess the secrets to overcoming negative circumstances, and they even try to explain the meaning and objective of death.

Furthermore, all religions claim to be owners of the truth and discredit the positions of others. Unfortunately, they try to conceive answers to the most profound questions of life without understanding truths of the Kingdom of God.

Some people have even concluded that all religions and spiritual paths can lead an individual to truth and a deeper connection with God. To them, all religions exist in a metaphorical "Commercial Center of Faith." One can choose his or her belief system based on personal preference. In that paradigm, Christianity is simply another "religious booth" promoting an option for spiritual enlightenment.

In truth, many people have the perception that Christianity is a religion because some Believers have misrepresented the faith by preaching rules and regulations instead of the message of the Kingdom. Because of the misrepresentations, some people have no interest in attending Christian services or following Christ. They do not understand that Believers represent a Heavenly government, not a religion.

My next statement may shock you, but I believe the term *Christian* is a misnomer for those who have embraced the Kingdom of God. Although people use the term "Christian" because they believe it is a positive title for those who follow Christ, the original use of the word was to mock those who had converted from Judaism to a belief in Christ (**Acts 11:26**). In my opinion, the most accurate name for Believers comes directly from the words of Jesus: *Sons of God* (**John 1:12**). The term *Kingdom Citizens* also accurately describes our relationship to God and the Kingdom. While some Believers may disagree with me on how we should identify ourselves, what is *most* important is that we understand that we represent the Kingdom that Jesus introduced.

Despite the tendency of people to label Believers as being part of the "Christian religion," the following chart highlights what I believe are key distinctions between religion and the Kingdom of God.

Concept	Perspective of Religion	Perspective of the Kingdom
Rules and Laws	Religion promotes man-made rules and rituals to appease God and to control the will and behavior of people.	The Supreme Laws of God include every precept, counsel, and guidance contained in His Word. God designed these Laws to establish order and to protect the Citizens of His Kingdom.
The Meaning of Life and Death	Religion teaches men to prepare to leave Earth in anticipation of a "better life" after death.	The Kingdom empowers people to live triumphantly while on Earth. Death is considered the end of a person's service to humanity. It should signify that the Believer has maximized his or her potential on Earth.
Personal Responsibility	Religion focuses on teaching Heaven, or the afterlife, as an escape from problems on Earth. It encourages people to act passively when facing life's circumstances instead of acting in a spirit of dominion.	In the Kingdom, individuals are empowered to solve problems and to be productive. The Kingdom encourages the individual to have a positive impact on the current and future generations.

Concept	Perspective of Religion	Perspective of the Kingdom
Relationship with God	Man seeks God through his methods.	God descends to Earth, in the form of Jesus, to engage with man and introduce him to the original Kingdom.
Heaven and Earth	God and the Kingdom reside in Heaven.	The Spirit of God lives in His people, and they bring Heaven's influence, culture, and rule to Earth. Jesus prayed, "Thy Kingdom Come." (Matthew 6:10)

As we can see in the chart, there is a significant difference between religion and the Kingdom of God! Those of us who believe in Jesus as their Lord and Savior are not religious; we are Citizens of His Kingdom. Jesus is a King; He is not a religious figure. The Bible refers to Him as, "KING OF KINGS, AND LORD OF LORDS" (Revelation 19:16). His Kingdom is for the here and now. It is not a promise for tomorrow; it is for today!

And despite attempts, no religion will ever be able to lead man to a relationship with God. Nor will any religion ever have the power to restore man back to his original place of dominion and wholeness. Wholeness and restoration only exist within the Kingdom of God.

If you are concerned that you have been taking part in religion instead of pursuing the Kingdom, take the time to meditate on the differences between religion and the Kingdom. You can also apply the following guidelines to make sure that your spiritual life is Kingdom-focused and not simply occupied by religious practices:

1. **Check Your Inner Man** – Do the beliefs and teachings you subscribe to resonate with the Spirit of God within you? Do you have peace in your heart that they reflect God's truth?

2. **Search the Scriptures** – Are the teachings you follow confirmed by Jesus' teachings as found in Scripture? Always search Scripture to verify that what you hear or what you believe is in God's Word. NEVER take a person's word for it. Just because someone stands behind a podium, does not mean they are prepared to share the TRUTH of God's Word. Likewise, just because you have formulated a certain perspective on life

because of your experiences does not mean that it aligns with the truths of the Kingdom.

3. **Be like the Bereans** – The surest way to distinguish between religious ideas and Kingdom principles is to know the Word of God. The Bereans were a group of Believers who the Apostle Paul describes as being diligent in their study and investigation of God's Word:

> *11 Now the Berean Jews were of more noble character than those in Thessalonica, for they received the message with great eagerness and examined the Scriptures every day to see if what Paul said was true. (Acts 17:11 NIV)*

THE RULES OF RELIGION VS. THE SUPREME LAW OF GOD

Some may argue that like religion, the Kingdom enforces a system of moral rules and regulations; this is one of many misunderstandings about the Kingdom. In actuality, the principles of the Kingdom, which include the Laws of God, exist to help us. They provide us with standards for living and promises that lead us to the path of success. They reveal how to prosper in family, business, career, health, personal development, service, and leadership:

> *8 This book of the law shall not depart out of thy mouth; but thou shalt meditate therein day and night, that thou mayest observe to do according to all that is written therein: for then thou shalt make thy way prosperous, and then thou shalt have good success. (Joshua 1:8)*

We are empowered to follow Kingdom principles, obey God, and overcome our shortcomings by confessing Jesus as our Lord and by honoring His sacrifice on the cross with the choices that we make:

> *9 That if thou shalt confess with thy mouth the Lord Jesus, and shalt believe in thine heart that God hath raised him from the dead, thou shalt be saved.*

> *10 For with the heart man believeth unto righteousness; and with the mouth confession is made unto salvation. (Romans 10:9-10)*

Some who have a religious mindset, only present the Laws of God as a tool to label and judge the sins of others. However, once a person enters the Kingdom, the salvation he receives guarantees that he is perfect, holy, and righteous in God's sight. His righteousness has nothing to do with his behavior, actions, or ability to keep the Law. That person can stand before God because the righteousness of Jesus Christ covers his short-comings and mistakes.

God established the Kingdom based on the desires and inclinations of His heart. If we do not understand God's heart, then we will read His Word as religious regulations, statutes, and rules designed to control and condemn us. The Laws of God are not about restriction. They are designed to help us live in a manner that will bring us the peaceful and fulfilled life that God intended. They help us to examine the desires of our hearts and show us how we can best honor God and love others:

> 7 The law of the Lord is perfect, converting the soul: the testimony of the Lord is sure, making wise the simple.
> 8 The statutes of the Lord are right, rejoicing the heart: the commandment of the Lord is pure, enlightening the eyes.
> 9 The fear of the Lord is clean, enduring for ever: the judgments of the Lord are true and righteous altogether.
> 10 More to be desired are they than gold, yea, than much fine gold: sweeter also than honey and the honeycomb.
> 11 Moreover by them is thy servant warned: and in keeping of them there is great reward.
> 12 Who can understand his errors? cleanse thou me from secret faults.
> 13 Keep back thy servant also from presumptuous sins; let them not have dominion over me: then shall I be upright, and I shall be innocent from the great transgression.
> 14 Let the words of my mouth, and the meditation of my heart, be acceptable in thy sight, O Lord, my strength, and my redeemer. (Psalm 19:7-14)

OLD COVENANT RITUALS VS. NEW COVENANT FULFILLMENT

Although the Kingdom of God is not a religion, I think it is important to discuss the purpose of the ritual sacrifices, traditions, and practices that God commanded His people to perform in the Old Testament. It is also important to address how Christ came to eliminate the need for these rituals and practices.

Before Christ came to Earth, God, through Moses, commanded the Israelites to observe certain practices (such as animal sacrifices) as a symbol of their covenant relationship with Him. These practices were designed to help God's people shape and align their morals, culture, and lifestyle with His ways; to acknowledge God's sovereignty and holiness; to engage in worship, thanksgiving, and atonement; and to demonstrate their overall consecration and commitment to Him.

> *1 And the Lord spake unto Moses and Aaron in the land of Egypt saying,*
> *2 This month shall be unto you the beginning of months: it shall be the first month of the year to you.*
> *3 Speak ye unto all the congregation of Israel, saying, In the tenth day of this month they shall take to them every man a lamb, according to the house of their fathers, a lamb for an house. (Exodus 12:1-3)*

> *5 Now therefore, if ye will obey my voice indeed, and keep my covenant, then ye shall be a peculiar treasure unto me above all people: for all the earth is mine:*
> *6 And ye shall be unto me a kingdom of priests, and an holy nation. These are the words which thou shalt speak unto the children of Israel. (Exodus 19:5-6)*

> *9 And he shall sprinkle of the blood of the sin offering upon the side of the altar; and the rest of the blood shall be wrung out at the bottom of the altar: it is a sin offering.*
> *10 And he shall offer the second for a burnt offering, according to the manner: and the priest shall make an atonement for him for his sin which he hath sinned, and it shall be forgiven him. (Leviticus 5:9-10)*

> *1 And the Lord spake unto Moses after the death of the two sons of Aaron, when they offered before the Lord, and died;*
> *2 And the Lord said unto Moses, Speak unto Aaron thy brother, that he come not at all times into the holy place within the vail before the mercy seat, which is upon the ark; that he die not: for I will appear in the cloud upon the mercy seat.*
> *3 Thus shall Aaron come into the holy place: with a young bullock for a sin offering, and a ram for a burnt offering. (Leviticus 16:1-3)*

Unfortunately, God knew that because of humanity's imperfection, that men and women would not be able to keep His laws and instructions. God, therefore, planned to relieve the burden of these laws and rituals by establishing a New Covenant with mankind. God desired to enter into a relationship with man that would not need to be maintained or affirmed by the performance of ritual sacrifices or the upholding of traditions. Through Jesus Christ (the Messiah), mankind would be able to freely fellowship, communicate, and worship a holy God despite man's human imperfections:

> *3 For what the law was powerless to do because it was weakened by the flesh, God did by sending his own Son in the likeness of sinful flesh to be a sin offering. And so he condemned sin in the flesh,*
> *4 In order that the righteous requirement of the law might be fully met in us, who do not live according to the flesh but according to the Spirit. (Romans 8:3-4 NIV)*

The writer to the Hebrews makes a very clear comparison between the Old Covenant and the New Covenant. The following scriptures will help us to learn and understand the fading away of the Old Covenant and the establishing of the New Covenant—to fully operate in the Earth through every Kingdom Citizen:

> *12 For I will be merciful to their unrighteousness, and their sins and their iniquities will I remember no more.*
> *13 In that he saith, A new covenant, he hath made the first old. Now that which decayeth and waxeth old is ready to vanish away. (Hebrews 8:12-13)*

> *1 For the law having a shadow of good things to come, and not the very image of the things, can never with those sacrifices which they offered year by year continually make the comers thereunto perfect.*
> *2 For then would they not have ceased to be offered? because that the worshippers once purged should have had no more conscience of sins.*
> *3 But in those sacrifices there is a remembrance again made of sins every year.*
> *4 For it is not possible that the blood of bulls and of goats should take away sins.*
> *5 Wherefore when he cometh into the world, he saith, Sacrifice and offering thou wildest not, but a body hast thou prepared me:*
> *6 In burnt offerings and sacrifices for sin thou hast had no pleasure.*
> *7 Then said I, Lo, I come (in the volume of the book it is written of me,) to do thy will, O God.*
> *8 Above when he said, Sacrifice and offering and burnt offerings and offering for sin thou wouldest not, neither hadst pleasure therein; which are offered by the law;*

9 Then said he, Lo, I come to do thy will, O God. He taketh away the first, that he may establish the second.

10 By the which will we are sanctified through the offering of the body of Jesus Christ once for all.

11 And every priest standeth daily ministering and offering oftentimes the same sacrifices, which can never take away sins:

12 But this man, after he had offered one sacrifice for sins for ever, sat down on the right hand of God;

13 From henceforth expecting till his enemies be made his footstool.

14 For by one offering he hath perfected for ever them that are sanctified. (Hebrews 10:1-14)

For many generations, God's people had heard the prophecies of the arrival of the Messiah and the establishment of the New Covenant:

14 Therefore the Lord himself shall give you a sign; Behold, a virgin shall conceive, and bear a son, and shall call his name Immanuel. (Isaiah 7:14)

6 For unto us a child is born, unto us a son is given: and the government shall be upon his shoulder: and his name shall be called Wonderful, Counsellor, The mighty God, The everlasting Father, The Prince of Peace. (Isaiah 9:6)

2 But thou, Bethlehem Ephratah, though thou be little among the thousands of Judah, yet out of thee shall he come forth unto me that is to be ruler in Israel; whose goings forth have been from of old, from everlasting. (Micah 5:2)

17 Thus there were fourteen generations in all from Abraham to David, fourteen from David to the exile to Babylon, and fourteen from the exile to the Messiah.

20 But after he had considered this, an angel of the Lord appeared to him in a dream and said, "Joseph son of David, do not be afraid to take Mary home as your wife, because what is conceived in her is from the Holy Spirit.

21 She will give birth to a son, and you are to give him the name Jesus, because he will save his people from their sins."

22 All this took place to fulfill what the Lord had said through the prophet:

23 "The virgin will conceive and give birth to a son, and they will call him Immanuel" (which means "God with us"). (Matthew 1:17, 20-23 NIV)

25 Now there was a man in Jerusalem called Simeon, who was righteous and devout. He was waiting for the consolation of Israel, and the Holy Spirit was on him.
26 It had been revealed to him by the Holy Spirit that he would not die before he had seen the Lord's Messiah.
27 Moved by the Spirit, he went into the temple courts. When the parents brought in the child Jesus to do for him what the custom of the Law required. (Luke 2:25-27 NIV)

But in the years between the Old and New Testament (the time between the books of **Malachi** and **Matthew**), while God's people waited for the arrival of the Messiah, several groups of religious authorities rose to positions of increased power and influence among the Jews. During that 400-year period, sometimes referred to as the "Silent Years," there was no direct word from God through the prophets, so these new religious authorities were left to interpret, instruct, and enforce God's laws and practices based on their counsel. The_Life Application Study Bible_ notes provide more insight on the spiritual leadership of that time:

> *Priests continue to provide leadership, but the people look to a new array of religious authorities as well, including Pharisees, Sadducees, and teachers of the law (also known as scribes). Overall, of these authorities sits a governing body called the Sanhedrin, which functions something like a religious Supreme Court.*
>
> *Most noticeable, perhaps, is the lack of prophets. Whereas Malachi had followed a succession of prophets going back hundreds of years, not a single divine spokesperson appeared before the nation during the years between the Old and New Testaments. . . For more than 400 years, the Heavens seemed closed to the nation of Israel. They heard nothing from God. Nothing but silence.*[2]

Unfortunately, by the time Jesus began His ministry, these groups of religious leaders had distorted the laws and practices instituted by God by adding to what He had already established. The religious leaders' distortions of God's laws and instructions did not enhance people's relationship with God; instead, they *increased* the people's spiritual burden:

> *7 Howbeit in vain do they worship me, teaching for doctrines the commandments of men.*

8 For laying aside the commandment of God, ye hold the tradition of men, as the washing of pots and cups: and many other such like things ye do. (Mark 7:7-8)

The birth of Jesus signified the arrival of the Messiah who came to fulfill the requirements of God's laws and rituals and to destroy all systems of manmade oppression, religion, and tradition. The *Life Application Study Bible* notes state:

> *[God's] silence ended. As Matthew opens his Gospel, the Jews are now unwilling subjects of the Roman empire. They are allowed freedom of worship and limited authority in overseeing their own affairs. But they long for more. They read the prophecies of the Old Testament and watch expectantly for the promised Messiah.[3]*

Through Jesus, man would have direct access to communicate and fellowship with God. Man would no longer need earthly priests to act as a mediator or ritual sacrifices to atone for sins. Christ Jesus would serve as mankind's eternal sacrifice and priest:

> *27 Unlike the other high priests, he does not need to offer sacrifices day after day, first for his own sins, and then for the sins of the people. He sacrificed for their sins once for all when he offered himself.*
> *28 For the law appoints as high priests men in all their weakness; but the oath, which came after the law, appointed the Son, who has been made perfect forever. (Hebrews 7:27-28 NIV)*
> *6 But in fact the ministry Jesus has received is as superior to theirs as the covenant of which he is mediator is superior to the old one, since the new covenant is established on better promises. (Hebrews 8:6 NIV)*

Once Jesus introduced the Kingdom on Earth, man no longer had to observe the **Old Covenant** rituals and practices to please God. Those who entered the Kingdom would have a heart reborn with God's Spirit and Word. They would have a heart that was genuinely motivated to live in a manner that pleased God:

> *3 You show that you are a letter from Christ, the result of our ministry, written not with ink but with the Spirit of the living God, not on tablets of stone but on tablets of human hearts. (2 Corinthians 3:3 NIV)*

It saddens me to see that some modern churches have begun to revive the Old Covenant practices such as festivals and rituals. What a tragedy! Jesus came to destroy this burden. The time has passed for the killing of animals in the temple and for observing the ancient practices of the Old Covenant. Jesus came to us to say, **"I am the final sacrifice; Learn from Me!"**

> *26 Otherwise Christ would have had to suffer many times since the creation of the world. But he has appeared once for all at the culmination of the ages to do away with sin by the sacrifice of himself. (Hebrews 9:26 NIV)*

CHOOSING THE KINGDOM OVER RELIGION:
THE STORY OF PAUL

Jesus desires for each of us to be part of the Kingdom, not religion. The Kingdom can accomplish what religion cannot: restoration of God's original intent for our lives. Even if we are under the control and influence of religion, when we encounter the Kingdom of God, we can experience spiritual freedom.

One of the most prominent examples of a person completely transformed by the Kingdom is the story of Saul of Tarsus—the man commonly known as Paul the Apostle. Before his encounter with Jesus, Paul was a true religious zealot. He fervently persecuted and tortured Believers for following Jesus. He believed that he was justified in his mission to preserve the teachings and practices of the Jewish Law:

> *13 For you have heard of my former conduct in Judaism, how I persecuted the church of God beyond measure and tried to destroy it.*
> *14 And I advanced in Judaism beyond many of my contemporaries in my own nation, being more exceedingly zealous for the traditions of my fathers. (Galatians 1:13-14 NKJV)*

Paul's encounter with Jesus brought a radical change to his perspective and ignited in him a righteous passion for the message of Jesus and the Kingdom:

> *18 Immediately, something like scales fell from Saul's eyes, and he could see again. He got up and was baptized,*
> *19 And after taking some food, he regained his strength. Saul spent several days with the disciples in Damascus.*

20 At once he began to preach in the synagogues that Jesus is the Son of God. (Acts 9:18-20 NIV)

Paul, the persecutor of the church, became a powerful man of God. After his transformation, he was so repentant of his old ways and developed such a love for sharing the truth of God's Word, people were no longer afraid of him. Instead of living in terror and hiding, they would gather in large crowds to hear him teach. The change in Paul was so great that he became one of the leading authorities on the Gospel of the Kingdom:

30 For two whole years Paul stayed there in his own rented house and welcomed all who came to see him.
31 He proclaimed the kingdom of God and taught about the Lord Jesus Christ—with all boldness and without hindrance! (Acts 28:30-31 NIV)

14 I myself am convinced, my brothers and sisters, that you yourselves are full of goodness, filled with knowledge and competent to instruct one another.
15 Yet I have written you quite boldly on some points to remind you of them again, because of the grace God gave me
16 To be a minister of Christ Jesus to the Gentiles. He gave me the priestly duty of proclaiming the gospel of God, so that the Gentiles might become an offering acceptable to God, sanctified by the Holy Spirit.
17 Therefore I glory in Christ Jesus in my service to God.
18 I will not venture to speak of anything except what Christ has accomplished through me in leading the Gentiles to obey God by what I have said and done—
19 By the power of signs and wonders, through the power of the Spirit of God. So from Jerusalem all the way around to Illyricum, I have fully proclaimed the gospel of Christ. (Romans 15:14-19 NIV)

Like Paul (before his transformation), many people are passionate and zealous for religion, but their passion is misguided. Their religious zeal brings no benefit to the lives of others. Their hearts are blind to what pleases God: building The Kingdom.

I recall the story of a man who attended Centro Diplomático. Before joining our congregation, he was a member of a religious organization (which I will refrain from naming). He had become increasingly dissatisfied with his spiritual development. He felt a sense of emptiness and knew that there was more to God and life.

While sitting in a religious gathering, the Spirit of the Lord spoke to him and told him to get up and run as far away from that organization as possible. The man left immediately. As he drove around town, the Spirit of God led him to Centro Diplomático. He had lived in the community for years but had never noticed our building or attended a service. When he arrived, he knew he was at the right place; we were teaching principles of the Kingdom of God. When he shared his testimony with the congregation, we were all amazed!

If your soul is hungry for the truth, God will guide you to it! Jesus says, **"Blessed are those who hunger and thirst for righteousness, for they will be filled"** (Matthew 5:6 NIV).

God says, **"And ye shall seek me, and find me, when ye shall search for me with all your heart"** (Jeremiah 29:13). When you develop a thirst and taste for the truth, your spirit will be so sensitive that you will recognize it as soon as you hear it. Encountering the truth will free you from religion and all manner of spiritual and emotional oppression. I encourage you to open your heart today and **learn from Jesus!**

KINGDOM REFLECTION

The Kingdom of God is not a religion. It is a Kingdom with a defined culture, leadership, and principles set up by God. Practicing religion is man's attempt to connect with God, but accepting Jesus Christ as one's Savior is the only way for man to enter into a relationship with God. Religion tries to explain the meaning of life, but it is only through the wisdom of the King that man can discover his place in God's Kingdom and discover truth.

KINGDOM ACTION

Some Believers have not had the opportunity to learn the truths of the Kingdom of God. They understand the concepts of salvation and redemption, and they know Christian traditions and practices, but they have no understanding of Kingdom principles. I would encourage anyone who is serious about learning the Kingdom to read the sermons, parables, and miracles of Jesus as documented in the Books of Matthew, Mark, Luke, John, and the Acts. As you **learn from Jesus**, I encourage you to assess your values, beliefs, and traditions. Be willing to exchange any religious idea for the truth of God's Word and His Kingdom:

> 14 But as for you, continue in what you have learned and have become convinced of, because you know those from whom you learned it,
> 15 And how from infancy you have known the Holy Scriptures, which are able to make you wise for salvation through faith in Christ Jesus.
> 16 All Scripture is God-breathed and is useful for teaching, rebuking, correcting and training in righteousness,
> 17 So that the servant of God may be thoroughly equipped for every good work. (2 Timothy 3:14-17 NIV)

Chapter 5

LEARNING TO TEACH THE MESSAGE
OF THE KINGDOM

In Jesus' first sermon, He proclaimed, **"Repent: for the kingdom of heaven is at hand"** (Matthew 4:17b). "At Hand," meant that the Kingdom was present and within reach. **Learning from Jesus** means we should learn to present the same message that He preached—the Kingdom.

In this chapter, we will learn:

- The importance of teaching the Kingdom message
- How Jesus made the Kingdom message His priority
- The problem with focusing on denomination and religion

MY ENCOUNTER WITH THE KINGDOM

In 1988, a dear friend lent me his copy of ***Paradise Restored: A Biblical Theology of Dominion***, written by David Chilton. This book completely opened my eyes to the purpose and power of the Kingdom. Not long after reading the book, I was in my office preparing a sermon. I stopped for a moment to watch a minister preaching on television. His sermon was so powerful that I began to take notes. He was speaking on discovering one's purpose and potential in the Kingdom of God. I had never heard anyone teach the Kingdom from that perspective. At the end of the broadcast, I ordered the minister's book. That minister was Dr. Myles Munroe. Two years after watching that broadcast, we at Centro Diplomático had the privilege of hosting Dr. Munroe at one of our Kingdom conferences.

On several occasions, Dr. Munroe testified that in his early years in the church, the subject of the Kingdom was not widely taught. With courage and humility, He acknowledged that after completing his seminary studies, he went out into the world to preach without the foundation of the Kingdom message. What a sad and tragic situation! Fortunately, he came to the knowledge of the Kingdom and went on to affect the lives of millions with the Kingdom message—including the parishioners at Centro Diplomático.

Although our current congregation at Centro Diplomático has a very strong foundation in the principles of the Kingdom, introducing the Kingdom message in 1988 had its challenges. At that time, the congregation had foundations in certain Biblical concepts and doctrines inherited from traditional Christianity. Many of the people had a belief system distorted by religiosity and tradition. I myself had taught on many subjects of the Bible, but I had not made the Kingdom the focus of my messages.

When I first presented the Kingdom message, I was very passionate in my approach. Unfortunately, the Kingdom was such a magnificent idea to grasp; many people felt overwhelmed by it. I decided to adjust my approach and introduce the subject gradually. Please notice that I did not say that I *stopped* teaching on the Kingdom. I simply modified my approach. I wanted to be sure that the message was clear and practical so the congregation could apply the teachings to their lives. In time, the congregation began to connect with the Kingdom teachings. And despite the challenging start, I praise God that many have since come to the knowledge of the Kingdom and have allowed its message to transform their lives.

It has been over 30 years since I realized that I made the serious error of not making the Kingdom of God the focus of our ministry at Centro Diplomático. Changing the focus of our ministry to the Kingdom was the best decision I could have made for myself, the congregation, my associate ministers, and my family.

I had to make the Kingdom message a priority for our ministry because it was the message that Jesus preached. I wanted to be obedient to the Lord's will. As followers of Jesus Christ, we should only teach the Kingdom message. We should not preach the ideologies of a denomination nor teach our traditions. If we want to lead people to the Kingdom, then we should teach the Kingdom! Keep reading there is more!

Jesus' priority was to introduce the Kingdom of God to humanity. During His first message, Jesus taught that the Kingdom of God was present and available to all: **"Repent: for the kingdom of heaven is at hand"** (**Matthew 4:17b**).

Jesus presented the Kingdom to people oppressed by the spiritual rule of religious leaders and the political rule of the Roman Empire. Jesus knew the people needed spiritual emancipation, empowerment, and elevation in their lives and way of thinking. They needed the good news of the Kingdom:

> *35 Jesus went through all the towns and villages, teaching in their synagogues, proclaiming the good news of the kingdom and healing every disease and sickness.*
> *36 When he saw the crowds, he had compassion on them, because they were harassed and helpless, like sheep without a shepherd. (Matthew 9:35-36 NIV)*

Although presenting the message of the Kingdom was Jesus' foremost concern, it is not the focus of some ministries today. Some teach a message of salvation, a message of prosperity, or a message of holiness, but they neglect to share the most important part of Jesus' message: the Kingdom of God.

It is time for us to rescue the teachings of Jesus! Every minister that stands before people has an obligation to give them the message of the Kingdom. Today, we have the opportunity to **learn from Jesus'** example and teach the message that was most important to Him: The Kingdom.

THE PROBLEM WITH FOCUSING ON DENOMINATION

There are many Christian denominations around the world—each with theological distinctions. Unfortunately, these denominations were born out of hundreds of years of debate and disagreement. Most denominations claim a belief in God, Jesus, and the Holy Spirit, and may even teach *certain* Kingdom concepts, but their doctrines lack the *central focus* of the Kingdom message.

Jesus did not present a religion or denomination. Preaching the Kingdom was His *mission* and *commission* to His disciples:

> 49 "For I did not speak on my own, but the Father who sent me commanded me to say all that I have spoken.
> 50 I know that his command leads to eternal life. So whatever I say is just what the Father has told me to say." (John 12:49-50 NIV)

Unfortunately, the religious leaders of Jesus' time were more concerned with upholding traditions and outward representations of religion than they were with opening their hearts to Jesus' Kingdom message and sharing that Word with God's people:

> 13 "Woe to you, teachers of the law and Pharisees, you hypocrites! You shut the door of the kingdom of heaven in people's faces. You yourselves do not enter, nor will you let those enter who are trying to. (Matthew 23:13 NIV)
> 27 Woe to you, teachers of the law and Pharisees, you hypocrites! You are like whitewashed tombs, which look beautiful on the outside but on the inside are full of the bones of the dead and everything unclean.
> 28 In the same way, on the outside you appear to people as righteous but on the inside you are full of hypocrisy and wickedness." (Matthew 23:27-28 NIV)

Just as the Pharisees received a warning about the danger of promoting religious practices, contemporary Believers should be careful not to promote religion or denomination because doing so would be a serious departure from the message that Jesus commanded us to teach.

Some denominations even preach Jesus as their central message; this too is incorrect. They emphasize and teach more on the *Jewish Jesus* than the *Eternal Christ*, who is still alive, present, and reigning in the 21st century. Jesus was the body through which Christ came and lived on Earth. When Jesus gave His life as a sacrifice for humanity, He finished the work that God assigned to Him. The Spirit of the Eternal Christ *carries on* the work of Jesus through the Church—His new body which consists of all Believers. The "Church" is an Embassy of the Kingdom of God, not a man-made religious organization. It is through the Church that Christ continues to take the message of the Kingdom of God to the entire world:

16 Therefore, from now on, we regard no one according to the flesh.
Even though we have known Christ according to the flesh, yet now we
know Him thus no longer. (2 Corinthians 5:16 NKJV)
11 So Christ himself gave the apostles, the prophets, the evangelists, the
pastors and teachers,
12 To equip his people for works of service, so that the body of Christ may
be built up
13 Until we all reach unity in the faith and in the knowledge of the Son of
God and become mature, attaining to the whole measure of the fullness
of Christ. (Ephesians 4:11-13 NIV)

Teaching on the personage and qualities of Jesus is wonderful. It is beautiful to want to honor the Lord Jesus in this way. However, if we neglect to share the message that He commanded us to teach, then we will not be following His instructions.

Before His crucifixion, Jesus charged His twelve disciples to make the message of the Kingdom a priority:

1 And when he had called unto him his twelve disciples, he gave them
power against unclean spirits, to cast them out, and to heal all manner
of sickness and all manner of disease.
2 Now the names of the twelve apostles are these; The first, Simon, who
is called Peter, and Andrew his brother; James the son of Zebedee, and
John his brother;
3 Philip, and Bartholomew; Thomas, and Matthew the publican; James
the son of Alphaeus, and Lebbaeus, whose surname was Thaddaeus;
4 Simon the Canaanite, and Judas Iscariot, who also betrayed him.
5 These twelve Jesus sent forth, and commanded them, saying, Go not
into the way of the Gentiles, and into any city of the Samaritans enter
ye not:
6 But go rather to the lost sheep of the house of Israel.
7 And as ye go, preach, saying, The kingdom of heaven is at hand.
(Matthew 10:1-7)

After His resurrection, Jesus' instructions to the disciples were the same. During the forty days before His ascension to Heaven, Jesus met with His disciples to prepare them to carry on His work. What did He share with them? His central theme was the Kingdom of God:

19 "Therefore go and make disciples of all nations, baptizing them in the
name of the Father and of the Son and of the Holy Spirit,

20 And teaching them to obey everything I have commanded you. And surely I am with you always, to the very end of the age." (Matthew 28:19-20 NIV)

The same commission that Jesus gave to His disciples is valid for us today. If we do not share Jesus' message, then we are not sharing His true philosophy. Even if we include Jesus in our theological perspectives, if our primary focus is not the Kingdom, then we are mistaken.

I understand that assigning a church a particular denomination may be necessary for legal purposes, but it pains me to see how much time we waste on presenting "doctrinal" messages that highlight denomination instead of the Kingdom. When we emphasize denomination, it means we have lost focus on the message that Jesus entrusted to us: that we now have the power of Heaven, that we have recovered our dominion on Earth, and that we have once again become conquerors in the Kingdom of God. The most certain plan for any ministry is to **learn from Jesus** and teach His Kingdom message!

THE CAGES OF DENOMINATION AND RELIGION

If we continue to focus on denomination, then we will neglect our obligation to share the holistic power of the Kingdom. Using a denomination as a point to persuade people to "join" a church or group is like trying to lock them in a spiritual cage. The Lord revealed this to me one afternoon while I was preparing a sermon. In my backyard, I have several fruit trees where birds love to gather. As I was studying, the birds were making so much noise I could not concentrate. I went outside to throw a few rocks at the tree to get the birds to fly away, but before I could throw the rocks, the Lord instructed me to stop. He told me that the birds were outdoors and in their domain. Because the birds were in their proper place, they were under His care:

25 Therefore I tell you, do not worry about your life, what you will eat or drink; or about your body, what you will wear. Is not life more than food, and the body more than clothes?
26 Look at the birds of the air; they do not sow or reap or store away in barns, and yet your heavenly Father feeds them. Are you not much more valuable than they?" (Matthew 6:25-26 NIV)

As I pondered what the Lord revealed to me about the birds in the trees, I thought about what happens to a bird captured in the wild. When a bird is in its natural habitat ("kingdom"), God is responsible for its well-being. Once that bird has been captured, caged, and removed from its rightful place, the responsibility of the bird's survival falls on the captor. God is no longer responsible for taking care of it.

It occurred to me that the birdcage is symbolic of what ministries do when they persuade people to join a congregation based on a denominational or religious message instead of the Kingdom message. It is as if they say, "Come to our religious group (Cage). We will feed you with" (fill in the blank with any one of the messages below):

- The Message of Prosperity
- The Message of Faith
- The Message of Healing
- The Message of Deliverance
- The Message of Correct Baptism
- The Message of Sound Doctrine
- The Message of Our Religion
- The Message of Our Denomination
- The Message of Entertainment (Instead of Training)

When a ministry tries to proselytize or "cage" people within a religious group or denomination, God no longer has an *obligation* to add *all things* to their lives; that religion or denomination takes on that responsibility:

> *31 Therefore take no thought saying, What shall we eat? or, What shall we drink? or, Wherewithal shall we be clothed?*
> *32 (For after all these things do the Gentiles seek:) for your heavenly Father knoweth that ye have need of all these things.*
> *33 But seek ye first the kingdom of God and his righteousness; and all these things shall be added unto you. (Matthew 6:31-33)*

God, out of His grace and love, supports all His children's needs, but He is only *responsible* for "adding all things" to those who first seek His Kingdom. His Kingdom ensures the integral prosperity of its Citizens—providing righteousness, joy, peace, health, and practical needs.

The religious leaders of Jesus' time attempted to "cage" Him in the same manner that some of our present-day denominations attempt to "cage" Believers and those who are seeking God. They wanted to confine Jesus' ministry to their religious constraints. When He healed someone on the Sabbath, the leaders interrogated Him about the "lawfulness" of His actions. On the days that He forgave people for their transgressions, the religious leaders wanted Him to use harsh judgment and a merciless application of the Law:

> *9 And when he was departed thence, he went into their synagogue:*
> *10 And, behold, there was a man which had his hand withered. And they asked him, saying, Is it lawful to heal on the sabbath days? that they might accuse him.*
> *11 And he said unto them, What man shall there be among you, that shall have one sheep, and if it fall into a pit on the sabbath day, will he not lay hold on it, and lift it out?*
> *12 How much then is a man better than a sheep? Wherefore it is lawful to do well on the sabbath days.*
> *13 Then saith he to the man, Stretch forth thine hand. And he stretched it forth; and it was restored whole, like as the other.*
> *14 Then the Pharisees went out, and held a council against him, how they might destroy him. (Matthew 12:9-14)*

> *21 And the scribes and the Pharisees began to reason, saying, Who is this which speaketh blasphemies? Who can forgive sins, but God alone?*
> *22 But when Jesus perceived their thoughts, he answering said unto them, What reason ye in your hearts?*
> *23 Whether is easier, to say, Thy sins be forgiven thee; or to say, Rise up and walk? (Luke 5:21-23)*

Despite the opposition and pressure of the religious leaders, Jesus never veered from His message.

Jesus did not speak about the Pentecostal, Marian, Apostolic or Baptist doctrine. The Kingdom was His primary focus. We should be like Jesus. Instead of inviting people to join a denomination, we should invite them to come and learn of the Kingdom: the place where they can find rest for their souls and where "**[all things are added unto every Believer]**" (**Matthew 6:33**).

The Lord made sure the apostles registered His instructions in the Bible for future generations to follow: to teach the Kingdom of God to the nations. Christ sent the gift of the Holy Spirit to ensure His disciples would possess boldness and power to share His message:

> 1 In my former book, Theophilus, I wrote about all that Jesus began to do and to teach
> 2 Until the day he was taken up to heaven, after giving instructions through the Holy Spirit to the apostles he had chosen.
> 3 After his suffering, he presented himself to them and gave many convincing proofs that he was alive. He appeared to them over a period of forty days and spoke about the kingdom of God.
>
> 8 But you will receive power when the Holy Spirit comes on you; and you will be my witnesses in Jerusalem, and in all Judea and Samaria, and to the ends of the earth." (Acts 1:1-3, 8 NIV)

Just like the apostles, all Believers have the support of the Holy Spirit, who dwells within. We each have the power and mandate from God to share the Kingdom message with the world. We should not allow minor issues such as denomination or religious creed to separate us. We should not **compete** with one another; we should **complete** the work of the Great Commission. Our focus should only be to teach the message of the Kingdom!

KINGDOM REFLECTION

Jesus did not come to preach denomination or religion. He came to teach the message of the Kingdom of God. We must prioritize the message of the Kingdom over denominational agendas and individual opinions. When we focus our message on denomination, we cheat ourselves and others out of experiencing the Kingdom message that the Son of God came to impart to humanity. But when we rescue the message of the Kingdom from traditionalism, we will be acting in obedience to the commission that Jesus gave to the disciples and to everyone who would follow Him.

KINGDOM CHALLENGE

Whether you are a **Pastor, Leader, or every day Believer** who wants to share your faith, I hope this chapter has inspired you to teach and share the good news of God's Kingdom. If you are unfamiliar with Kingdom teachings, ask the Lord to guide your studies and give you a revelation of the Kingdom so that your words and life will be a reflection of its authenticity and power.

The Apostle Peter offered the following advice on sharing one's faith:

> *But in your hearts revere Christ as Lord. Always be prepared to give an answer to everyone who asks you to give the reason for the hope that you have. But do this with gentleness and respect. (I Peter 3:15 NIV)*

Believers should always be prepared to discuss the Kingdom with humility and love. Ask the Lord to give you the boldness, wisdom, words, and gentleness to share His message. Your testimony of encountering the Kingdom will encourage others to seek its truth, power, and privileges.

PICTURES... VISUAL ILLUSTRATION OF JESUS'S KINGDOM TEACHING

Notes on the Cages of Religion, Denomination, and Government

25 "Therefore I say to you, do not worry about your life, what you will eat or what you will drink; nor about your body, what you will put on. Is not life more than food and the body more than clothing?
26 Look at the birds of the air, for they neither sow nor reap nor gather into barns; yet your heavenly Father feeds them. Are you not of more value than they?"
(Matthew 6:25-26 NKJV)

33 But seek first the kingdom of God and His righteousness, and all these things shall be added to you. (Matthew 6:33 NKJV)

The image above illustrates the message Jesus preached in **Matthew 6:25-26.** God faithfully takes care of His creation, whether the lilies of the fields or the birds of the air. God feeds them, looks after them, and makes sure that they thrive in their habitat.

God created birds to be free, to fly, and to exist and find food without worry. But as you can see in the image below, when men capture and put birds in cages, they inherit the responsibility of feeding and caring for them.

Just like the birds of the air, God promised His people that if they would seek His Kingdom first, He would take care of all their needs and ensure that nothing would be lacking from their lives.

However, when a person joins a religious organization, and that religion manipulates and "cages" that man or woman with rules, regulations, and ideas, it can hinder that person from experiencing the care, security, and benefits of God's Kingdom. That man or woman becomes subject to the "care" and control of that religion just like captured birds become the responsibility of their captors. Instead of teaching people how to pray, access Kingdom power, and exercise dominion over their circumstances, religious leaders encourage people to be dependent upon them for prayer.

And instead of teaching people to seek God's direction to discover the true purpose for their gifts, religious leaders burden their parishioners with activities and programs that lead people to experience frustration, unfulfilled potential, exhaustion, and resentment.

The same type of "caging" also occurs in certain governments. There are many nations throughout the world that enforce oppressive and inhumane laws to control their citizens. That should not be so!

While a government should have the right to hold individuals accountable for inappropriate conduct or for violating the laws of the nation and the rights of other citizens, a government *should not* control the God-given right of a person to live a quality life.

A government *should* only control the discovery and management of the land's natural resources (such as minerals, gold, silver, or oil) and use those resources to create economic opportunities that will enable the citizens to live free, productive, and prosperous lives.

God never intended for mankind to be caged, controlled, or manipulated by any system, whether religious or governmental.

His original plan was for all people to be free to dream and have a vision for their lives, to serve Him with their gifts, to maximize their potential and live free of limitations, to be a blessing to others, and to make a positive difference in the world.

God intended for us to experience a life of abundance, power, and happiness. Our lives should be as liberated and secure as the birds of the air: free from worry, free to fly, and free to enjoy the good things that Our Creator provides.

Be free to live, to think, to dream, and to succeed!

There are no limits to what you can achieve. You can go as far as your eyes can see and beyond!

Go Ahead and Enjoy the Glorious Benefits of the Kingdom of God!

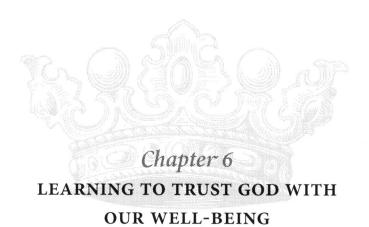

Chapter 6
LEARNING TO TRUST GOD WITH
OUR WELL-BEING

Learning from Jesus can give us assurance that God cares about our physical, emotional, and spiritual well-being. When we trust the Lord with our lives, we can have faith that He will provide for our daily needs, that He will strengthen and preserve us in times of crisis, and that He will give us peace and wisdom to triumph over the storms of life.

In this chapter, we will learn:

- How to trust God to provide for our needs
- How to trust God to support our physical, emotional, and spiritual wellness
- How to trust God to sustain us in times of difficulty

KINGDOM PROVISION

When my son was born, I wanted to be a good father and take care of him to the best of my ability. I believe that my desire to care for my son reflected the same love that God has for His children. He wants the best for us. He knows what we need and makes sure that we have the resources to fulfill those needs.

One of the lessons that Jesus taught during His "Sermon on the Mount" encouraged people *to trust* God to meet their needs instead of *worrying about* their needs:

25 Therefore I tell you, do not worry about your life, what you will eat or drink; or about your body, what you will wear. Is not life more than food, and the body more than clothes?
26 Look at the birds of the air; they do not sow or reap or store away in barns, and yet your heavenly Father feeds them. Are you not much more valuable than they?
27 Can any one of you by worrying add a single hour to your life?
...
31 So do not worry, saying, 'What shall we eat?' or 'What shall we drink?' or 'What shall we wear?'
32 For the pagans run after all these things, and your heavenly Father knows that you need them.
33 But seek first his kingdom and his righteousness, and all these things will be given to you as well. (Matthew 6:25-27, 31-33 NIV)

Finding support for our needs is one of the promises that we inherit in the Kingdom of God. Dr. Myles Munroe taught that one of the key characteristics of a kingdom is that it functions as a Commonwealth and supports its citizens. In *Rediscovering the Kingdom*, he says the following:

A Commonwealth is an economic system which guarantees each citizen equal access to financial security. In a kingdom, the term commonwealth is used because the king's desire is that all his citizens share and benefit from the wealth of the kingdom. The kingdom's glory is in the happiness and health of its citizens.[1]

If an Earthly king can design a system that attends to the needs of its people, then how much more can the **King of Kings** and **His Kingdom** provide for His Citizens?

While ministering on Earth, Jesus always demonstrated confidence in God as His provider. There were several accounts in the Bible when God provided Jesus and the disciples with what they needed for survival and to minister to others:

24 After Jesus and his disciples arrived in Capernaum, the collectors of the two-drachma temple tax came to Peter and asked, "Doesn't your teacher pay the temple tax?"
25 "Yes, he does," he replied. When Peter came into the house, Jesus was the first to speak. "What do you think, Simon?" he asked. "From whom do the kings of the earth collect duty and taxes—from their own children or from others?"

26 "From others," Peter answered. "Then the children are exempt," Jesus said to him.
27 "But so that we may not cause offense, go to the lake and throw out your line. Take the first fish you catch; open its mouth and you will find a four-drachma coin. Take it and give it to them for my tax and yours."
(Matthew 17:24-27 NIV)

Jesus was never anxious about any of His needs. He knew that if He were doing God's will, His Father would provide Him access to the provisions of Heaven. Jesus' example should give us great peace. When we feel overwhelmed by the pressures of life, we should have confidence that God is aware of our needs and that He will provide us with a means to fulfill those needs:

19 But my God shall supply all your need according to his riches in glory by Christ Jesus. (Philippians 4:19)

Jesus teaches us to ask God for what we need and believe that He has already answered our prayers:

22 And all things, whatsoever ye shall ask in prayer, believing, ye shall receive. (Matthew 21:22)

We can receive the answers to our prayers either through the generosity of others, or God will give instructions on how to obtain what we need:

17 Even so faith, if it hath not works, is dead, being alone. (James 2:17)

We should **learn from Jesus** and *know* that God will always take care of His Children.

PROVIDING PEACE

In the Kingdom, we find provisions for our everyday needs as well as the intangible blessings that ensure the well-being of our souls: joy, peace, emotional stability, and clarity of mind. The Apostle Paul confirms this in the **Book of Romans** when he states, **"For the kingdom of God is not meat and drink; but righteousness, and peace, and joy in the Holy Ghost."** (Romans 14:17)

A few years ago, I received a telephone call that was very disturbing. I was in such a state of distress from the news I had received, I developed muscle spasms, my back began to ache, and I felt a knot form in my neck. My peace disappeared, and my soul lost its rest. I was in severe pain, and I could not think straight. I could feel myself entering a state of extreme anxiety. I knew I could not solve the problem in that state, so I went home for the day to calm my nerves and quiet my soul. Eventually, the Spirit of God revealed the solution to me! I regained my peace, and my body began to function normally.

Panic, anxiety, and worry will never help us solve our problems. They only diminish our confidence in the Lord and disrupt our peace. However, when we choose to hold onto our peace and seek the Lord for wisdom, we can gain insight on how to manage challenging situations, and we can preserve our health. We save ourselves from the damage that stress and worry can have on our bodies as well as our minds.

The Lord never intended for us to feel overwhelmed or disturbed by our problems. Our peace is His priority. Jesus said if we **Learn from Him** we will find rest for our souls:

> 4 *Rejoice in the Lord always. I will say it again: Rejoice!*
> 5 *Let your gentleness be evident to all. The Lord is near.*
>
> 6 *Do not be anxious about anything, but in every situation, by prayer and petition, with thanksgiving, present your requests to God.*
> 7 *And the peace of God, which transcends all understanding, will guard your hearts and your minds in Christ Jesus. (Philippians 4:4-7 NIV)*

THE IMPORTANCE OF PHYSICAL REST

God cares for our mental well-being as well as the health of our bodies, especially as it pertains to us getting the proper amount of physical rest.

Have you ever been so tired that even when you tried to sleep, you were not able? That level of fatigue and exhaustion usually results from being physically or emotionally overwhelmed. Sometimes Believers overexert themselves and do not take the time to recharge. That is not the correct way to live.

In the **Book of Genesis**, we see that even the Creator of the universe rested from His work:

> 2 And on the seventh day God ended his work which he had made; and he rested on the seventh day from all his work which he had made.
> 3 And God blessed the seventh day, and sanctified it: because that in it he had rested from all his work which God created and made. (Genesis 2:2-3)

I emphasize the importance of rest because Jesus emphasized it. In **Mark 6:31,** Jesus encouraged His disciples to rest. He acknowledged that they had been working hard at serving people. Naturally, they were tired, so He invited them to recuperate their strength in a quiet and peaceful place:

> 31 And he said unto them, Come ye yourselves apart into a desert place, and rest a while: for there were many coming and going, and they had no leisure so much as to eat.

Although physical rest is essential for our health, some people still overwork themselves. The demand they put on their bodies exceeds the proper limits. They feel guilty about taking the time to rest and ignore the warning signs that their bodies are fatigued.

There are many reasons why people do not have the proper balance of work and rest, but below are several that I believe are most prevalent:

1. They are exhausted because they try to pacify their conscience or fulfill an obligation to God by involving themselves in too many church activities and services. They believe that overexertion for the sake of the church is a sign of spirituality and righteousness. They *think* that their busyness pleases the Lord, but in reality, they are only overwhelming the temple of God (their bodies). They do not realize that there is a difference between working hard and pushing one's body beyond what is reasonable.

2. They are fatigued because they preoccupy themselves with activities that have no relationship to their gifts and have no *Kingdom relevance.* When people try to function in a capacity that does not fit God's design and plan for them, it can cause fatigue and exhaustion because it is a misuse of their energy and talents.

3. They do not get enough rest because they are afraid that no one else can perform a job or task to their standards. So, they refuse to ask for help.

4. They spend more time *doing the work of the Lord* rather than *spending time with the Lord of the work*. Some ministers and leaders focus so heavily on planning programs and conferences that they put their health, and even their families, at risk. They neglect to spend time studying the Word and fellowshipping with the Holy Spirit who could help them adjust their focus and give them wisdom on how to effectively and efficiently carry out the work of the Kingdom.

5. They do not know how to manage their time and resources properly so that they are less tired but more productive.

Whatever the cause, a lack of rest can be as detrimental to our bodies as a lack of food and water. God designed the human body to replenish and renew itself during the hours that we sleep. Clearly, rest is essential!_
Someone once said there are times in the life of a disciple when the most spiritual thing he can do is rest. When we wear ourselves down, we cease to be effective. Fatigue can cause us to be irritable, make bad decisions, and even treat others poorly.

We should not only be mindful of our need for rest, but we should also encourage our loved ones to get rest. If we know someone is exhausted and overworked, then we should tell them, "*You have worked hard; you need to stop and rest.*"

The greatest secret to achieving efficiency in our lives is to have Jesus as our partner. When we consult the Lord on the management of our responsibilities, our lives have increased organization and productivity, and our personal affairs come into order.

REST FROM EMOTIONAL WEARINESS

Emotional weariness is a very real phenomenon. I have noted what I believe are some causes of emotional weariness:

1. **Challenging Circumstances** - Some people are exhausted due to the trials of life. They have experienced extremely difficult circumstances and

have lost their sense of hope and joy. Others have no inner peace because they are exhausted from battling personal challenges. Some people are so emotionally overwhelmed, they have considered taking their own lives. They simply do not have the strength to bear their problems. Whatever the cause, emotional weariness can keep people from experiencing the serene life that God promises to those who follow Him:

> 28 *"Come to me, all you who are weary and burdened, and I will give you rest.*
> 29 *Take my yoke upon you, and learn from me, for I am gentle and humble in heart, and you will find rest for your souls.*
> 30 *For my yoke is easy and my burden is light." (Matthew 11:28-30 NIV)*

2. Religion - Some Believers are weary because they have not accessed the wisdom and peace of the Kingdom. They have only tried to handle their problems by relying on the ineffective ideas of religious systems. The term "ineffective ideas" refers to any religious concepts that do not agree with what Jesus taught. Religious teachings undermine people's ability to embrace Kingdom principles and inhibit them from experiencing the abundant and high-quality life that God promises to Believers:

> 10 *The thief cometh not, but for to steal, and to kill, and to destroy: I am come that they might have life, and that they might have it more abundantly. (John 10:10)*

Who is John referring to as the *thief*? If we read a few verses above, Jesus explains in **verse 8** that the thief symbolizes the oppressive religious systems that came before Him. If we are not careful, religious traditions and practices can rob us of the peace that the Kingdom affords us:

> 8 *All that ever came before me are thieves and robbers: but the sheep did not hear them.*
> 9 *I am the door: by me if any man enter in, he shall be saved, and shall go in and out, and find pasture. (John 10:8-9)*

> 13 *But woe unto you, scribes and Pharisees, hypocrites! for ye shut up the kingdom of heaven against men: for ye neither go in yourselves, neither suffer ye them that are entering to go in.*

15 Woe unto you, scribes and Pharisees, hypocrites! for ye compass sea and land to make one proselyte, and when he is made, ye make him twofold more the child of hell than yourselves. (Matthew 23:13, 15)

3. Self-reliance – Some people are weary because they are too proud to admit (even to God) that they need help with their problems. They do not realize that God never intended for us to face our trials or carry our burdens in our human strength. God wants for us to take control of situations by relying on *His* power and wisdom that reside within us:

1 God is our refuge and strength, a very present help in trouble. (Psalm 46:1)

6 Humble yourselves, therefore, under God's mighty hand, that he may lift you up in due time.
7 Cast all your anxiety on him because he cares for you. (1 Peter 5:6-7 NIV)

The Holy Spirit dwells within each Believer and is available to counsel us on how to manage our circumstances:

13 But when he, the Spirit of truth, comes, he will guide you into all the truth. He will not speak on his own; he will speak only what he hears, and he will tell you what is yet to come. (John 16:13 NIV)

4. Depression - Some people have emotional weariness caused by depression. The root of their depression could be physical illness, hormonal imbalance, grief (due to the loss of a loved one), loss of employment, financial hardships, or other reasons. Depression is a very serious matter. If you think you are experiencing depression, please do not be afraid or ashamed to seek professional help. As you seek a path to wellness, I urge you to reach out to supportive Believers who will walk with you through this valley in your life so you can once again experience joy.

My wife and I own and operate the KNC Nutritional Center in El Monte, CA. The Center offers education, services, and support for the health of all components of the human system: body, mind, and soul. Through my work at KNC, I have come to understand that it is important for people to take care of their physical, emotional, and spiritual health. God designed these three parts of a human being to work in harmony. But if a person is suffering in one of the three areas, it can negatively affect the others and throw his or her total well-being out of balance.

When people feel overwhelmed by their circumstances and seek help, they need to hear the voice of Jesus Christ reach out to them through the Church: *"Are you upset? Do you feel burdened? Are you afraid? Do you want to give up on life? Come to your Creator."* The Lord is calling all who are weary to come to Him. No matter the issue or the cause of the weariness, Jesus says, **"Come to me, all you who are weary"** (Matthew 11:28a NIV). What a miraculous invitation!

A PRESENT HELP IN TIMES OF TROUBLE

On more than one occasion, Jesus came to the aid of His disciples to help them overcome difficult circumstances. We can look to these accounts to gain insight into how Jesus desires Believers to respond to life's difficulties.

Let us examine **Matthew 14:22-29b:**

> *22 Immediately Jesus made the disciples get into the boat and go on ahead of him to the other side, while he dismissed the crowd.*
> *23 After he had dismissed them, he went up on a mountainside by himself to pray. Later that night, he was there alone,*
> *24 And the boat was already a considerable distance from land, buffeted by the waves because the wind was against it.*
> *25 Shortly before dawn Jesus went out to them, walking on the lake.*
> *26 When the disciples saw him walking on the lake, they were terrified. "It's a ghost," they said, and cried out in fear.*
> *27 But Jesus immediately said to them: "Take courage! It is I. Don't be afraid."*
> *28 "Lord, if it's you," Peter replied, "tell me to come to you on the water."*
> *29 "Come," he said. Then Peter got down out of the boat, walked on the water and came toward Jesus. (NIV)*

During His prayer time, Jesus realized that something in the natural world needed His attention. The close intimacy He shared with God enabled Him to discern that there was trouble. The disciples were in the midst of a powerful storm. They were in a state of panic and were afraid of perishing. It was at that moment that Jesus walked on water toward the ship and said to Peter, **"*Come.*"** Peter obeyed Jesus' command. By doing so, Peter did more than walk on water, he walked on the WORD OF JESUS: *"Come."* The command of Jesus, *"Come,"* has particular depth. Every time we communicate with the Lord and raise questions or concerns of any kind about our life, He tells us, *"Come."* Through God, we can obtain power and wisdom to face and subdue any storms that arise in our lives. In Him, we have complete security. In times of trouble, we should not turn to people or religion, we should, *"Come"* to Jesus Christ!

KEEPING OUR EYES ON JESUS CHRIST

When Peter responded to the call of Jesus, he fixed his eyes on Him. Peter took the first steps on the water without incident. He did not sink in the waves nor was he knocked down by the wind. However, once he took his eyes off Jesus and looked at the storm, the real trouble began:

> *29 Then Peter got down out of the boat, walked on the water and came toward Jesus.*
> *30 But when he saw the wind, he was afraid and, beginning to sink, cried out, "Lord save me!" (Matthew 14:29b-30 NIV)*

This passage holds a very important teaching: Peter only became afraid when he allowed the wind and waves to distract his focus from Jesus. Peter's faith faltered when he began to focus more on the surrounding storm than on the ability of the Lord to *guide him through* the storm.
Just like Peter, when we face challenges, we must first obey the Word of the Lord, "Come." We need to allow Him to guide us safely to the other side of the storm. We cannot let the storm intimidate, distress, or distract us from trusting the words of Jesus and obeying Him completely.

When Peter began to sink and cry out for help, what was the Lord's response? He did not rebuke Peter for looking at the waves, nor did He say to him, "Swallow a little more water so that you will learn a lesson about doubting Me." Rather, Jesus took Peter by the hand and lifted him up from the waves so he would not drown. When Jesus and Peter returned to the boat, the winds calmed. The disciples worshipped the Lord saying, "Truly you are the Son of God."

On a similar occasion, Jesus and the disciples got on a boat to cross the Sea of Galilee. Once again, a strong wind began to agitate the boat. The disciples were desperate and full of fear. Instead of speaking to the storm themselves, they immediately awakened Jesus who was asleep at the bottom of the ship:

25 And his disciples came to him, and awoke him, saying, Lord, save us: we perish.
26 And he saith unto them, Why are ye fearful, O ye of little faith? Then he arose and rebuked the winds and the sea; and there was a great calm. (Matthew 8:25-26)

A modern interpretation of Jesus' response to the disciples, might read, **"You have already been taught; you are in a condition to act. Why did you awaken me?"** Jesus chastised the disciples for having *little faith* because they had not put into practice what He had taught them about how to handle a storm. Despite Jesus' disappointment in their lack of faith, He spoke and calmed the storm.

No matter how many times Jesus had delivered the disciples from difficulties in the past, the storm still rattled them. His ability to calm the wind and waves still surprised them. What was the reaction of the disciples after Jesus took command of the storm? The Scripture reveals that they were amazed: **"But the men marvelled saying, What manner of man is this, that even the winds and the sea obey him!"** (Matthew 8:27).

We are sometimes like the disciples. We need the Lord to deliver us from trouble many times before we learn to respond to our storms with an attitude of faith and confidence instead of fear and dread. When will we stop *reacting* to our problems and start *responding* to our situations in *faith?* When will we use the *Word* that we have already *heard?* When will we mature from being *surprised* by His power to *expecting* the Lord's power to manifest?

No matter the circumstances, you must focus on Jesus Christ and His Word. If you do this, no wind can stop you. Fear will not be able to detain you. Nothing will be able to turn you aside. There will always be storms, waves, and wind in your life. If they distract you, you will surely sink. However, if you are faithful to the instructions found in God's Word, even if you face fierce winds and mighty waves, you will have peace. You will know without a doubt that **Jesus Christ is present on the inside of you and willing to help you through every challenging circumstance.**

Kingdom Citizens should be confident that we have the support of the King. Whether it is an emotional or physical need, we are never without His presence and power. For He promised, **"Lo, I am with you alway, even unto the end of the world. Amen"** (Matthew 28:20b).

God promises His Citizens a life of abundance:

> *10 The thief cometh not, but for to steal, and to kill, and to destroy: I am come that they might have life, and that they might have it more abundantly. (John 10:10)*

The word "life" translates to "Zoe" in Greek. Zoe means a high quality and long-lasting (durable) life. God established His Kingdom as a commonwealth system to ensure His Citizens would experience this high-quality life and have access to provisions to fulfill their practical and spiritual needs.

Jesus exemplified ultimate confidence in God as His provider. We can draw peace from Jesus' example and trust that God has already provided for all our needs and desires. We can always depend on the Lord to support us during difficult times. Jesus' prescription for our stress, weariness, and anxiety is for us to **Come to Him, Learn from Him,** and **Find rest** for our souls. Whether He performs a miracle on our behalf or gives us the courage and wisdom to handle our situations, God will always be present to help us to triumph because He lives inside of us.

KINGDOM CHALLENGE

Do you trust God for your needs? Do you worry and doubt during times of trouble? The following scriptures will help you increase your faith in God as your provider and Lord:

> *6 Do not be anxious about anything, but in every situation, by prayer and petition, with thanksgiving, present your requests to God. (Philippians 4:6 NIV)*

> *19 And my God will meet all your needs according to the riches of his glory in Christ Jesus." (Philippians 4:19 NIV)*

> *3 You will keep in perfect peace those whose minds are steadfast, because they trust in you." (Isaiah 26:3 NIV)*

> *1 The Lord is my shepherd; I shall not want. (Psalm 23:1)*

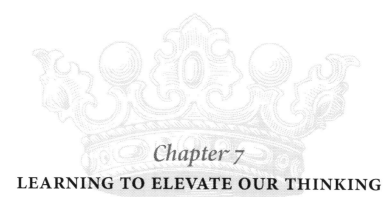

Chapter 7
LEARNING TO ELEVATE OUR THINKING

No matter the lesson we **learn from King Jesus**, it will always require a change in our behavior, and more importantly, an elevation in our thinking. Our level of thinking is one of the factors that will decide whether we experience the blessings that come from applying Jesus' teachings.

If you have ever visited or worked in a high-rise building, you may have noticed that the employees who possess the most authority tend to work in offices on the upper floors. The quickest way to access those floors would be to take the elevator. What is most important in this example is not *who* works on the upper floors of the building, but *how* you would access those floors — the elevator.

Let us relate this example to life in the Kingdom of God. The benefits of the Kingdom—identity, purpose, and power—exist on the inside of each of us. However, we need an internal "mechanism" that will help us to access our Kingdom characteristics and privileges. That mechanism is our way of thinking. If we want to experience the power and benefits of the Kingdom, our thoughts must align with Kingdom principles.

Jesus was successful in fulfilling His mission on Earth because He kept a strict focus on the Kingdom. His thoughts, words, and actions were a direct reflection of the Kingdom's influence. When we **learn from Jesus** and choose to elevate our thinking, we can experience the transformed and abundant life that God has promised His Children:

8 Finally, brothers and sisters, whatever is true, whatever is noble, whatever is right, whatever is pure, whatever is lovely, whatever is admirable—if anything is excellent or praiseworthy—think about such things. (Philippians 4:8 NIV)

In this chapter, we will learn:

- How our thinking impacts the state of our lives
- The importance of renewing our minds with God's Word
- How to combat negative thoughts and elevate our thinking so that our lives can ascend to new levels in the Kingdom of God

RENEWING THE MIND

Before Jesus came to Earth, the prophets declared that His presence would bring deliverance, healing, and freedom—all of which are benefits of the Kingdom of God. Although these benefits are *available* to us today, many Believers suffer silently because they have not *experienced* these benefits. They have not experienced Kingdom benefits because they have not renewed their minds with the Word of God.

Negative thinking can prevent us from understanding what is available to us in the Kingdom. If our thinking (the elevator) is not functioning properly, then it will not take us to the higher levels of life that we have the potential to reach. Instead, our lives will remain stagnant.

Just like elevators require periodic maintenance, repair, and even a complete refurbishment to ensure their functionality, it is important that we refresh our minds, our perspectives, and our meditations to ensure that our thoughts are helping us to experience the fullness of life in God's Kingdom.

Renewing the mind is a necessary undertaking. God did not design our souls to stay in an underdeveloped state; He intended for us to reach greater levels of maturity. We can only experience spiritual development when we increase our knowledge and understanding of God and His Word:

2 And be not conformed to this world: but be ye transformed by the renewing of your mind, that ye may prove what is that good, and acceptable, and perfect, will of God. (Romans 12:2)

22 You were taught, with regard to your former way of life, to put off your old self, which is being corrupted by its deceitful desires;
23 To be made new in the attitude of your minds;
24 And to put on the new self, created to be like God in true righteousness and holiness. (Ephesians 4:22-24 NIV)

What wonderful counsel from the Holy Spirit to every Believer!

Once we enter the Kingdom, renewing the mind becomes essential to manifesting our Kingdom potential. The process of developing our minds and souls may take time, but a change in our thinking will take place:

18 But we all, with open face beholding as in a glass the glory of the Lord, are changed into the same image from glory to glory, even as by the Spirit of the Lord. (2 Corinthians 3:18)

FEEDING THE MIND

Elevation of our thinking can only occur if we nourish our minds and souls with the Word of God. The subconscious mind feeds and meditates on the ideas that we take in. It does not matter if the thoughts are positive or negative; the mind does not discriminate. The only way for us to develop Kingdom thinking is to fill our minds with the Word of God:

16 All scripture is given by inspiration of God, and is profitable for doctrine, for reproof, for correction, for instruction in righteousness:
17 That the man of God may be perfect, thoroughly furnished unto all good works. (2 Timothy 3:16-17)

4 But he answered and said, It is written, Man shall not live by bread alone, but by every word that proceedeth out of the mouth of God. (Matthew 4:4)

2 As newborn babes, desire the sincere milk of the word, that ye may grow thereby. (I Peter 2:2)

The same Word of God that created the Heavens and the Earth is the same Word of God that has the power to create a new life within each of us. It is the key to transforming the environment of our minds from negative and destructive to positive and flourishing. The Apostle John affirms, "**The**

Word that gives life was from the beginning, and this is the one our message is about" (I John 1:1 Contemporary English Version).

God's Word gives us the power to conquer thoughts that are contrary to Kingdom principles:

> *4 (For the weapons of our warfare are not carnal, but mighty through God to the pulling down of strong holds;)*
> *5 Casting down imaginations, and every high thing that exalteth itself against the knowledge of God, and bringing into captivity every thought to the obedience of Christ. (2 Corinthians 10:4-5)*

We can overcome carnal, unproductive, and harmful thinking but we must commit to the renewal process. In **Matthew 11:12**, we read, **"And from the days of John the Baptist until now the kingdom of heaven suffereth violence, and the violent take it by force."** There have been many interpretations of this verse. My interpretation is that "violence" does not refer to physical force but rather the level of intensity and determination that we need to apply to become a complete realization of who God intended us to be. It means we should invest maximum effort in the study and application of God's Word so that our minds will have the power to overcome thoughts that would hinder our growth.

For example, when we have thoughts that encourage fear, we should meditate on scriptures that foster courage and faith: **"For God hath not given us the spirit of fear; but of power, and of love, and of a sound mind"** (2 Timothy 1:7).

When we have thoughts that demean our sense of worth, we should find a scripture that affirms our identity and significance in the Kingdom:

> *9 But ye are a chosen generation, a royal priesthood, an holy nation, a peculiar people; that ye should shew forth the praises of him who hath called you out of darkness into his marvellous light. (1 Peter 2:9)*

Elevating our thinking may be a slow and challenging process, but we must be consistent in feeding our minds with the Word so that it will dominate our thinking and give us the power to combat harmful thoughts. We will know that our thinking has experienced elevation when our thoughts motivate us to believe and act according to Kingdom principles and the Word of God.

A KINGDOM STATE OF MIND

Jesus Christ is the best example of someone who had a Kingdom-focused mind. Even at an early age, Jesus had one agenda: to serve the will and interest His Father's Kingdom. He did not allow external or internal challenges to distract Him from His path:

> *39 Going a little farther, he fell with his face to the ground and prayed, "My Father, if it is possible, may this cup be taken from me. Yet not as I will, but as you will." (Matthew 26:39 NIV)*

Even when challenged by the religious leaders, Jesus never lost confidence or got off course from what He was assigned to do:

> *46 And it came to pass, that after three days they found him in the temple, sitting in the midst of the doctors, both hearing them, and asking them questions.*
> *47 And all that heard him were astonished at his understanding and answers.*
> *48 And when they saw him, they were amazed: and his mother said unto him, Son, why hast thou thus dealt with us? behold, thy father and I have sought thee sorrowing.*
> *49 And he said unto them, How is it that ye sought me? wist ye not that I must be about my Father's business. (Luke 2:46-49)*

The Apostle Paul also describes Jesus as having an unrelenting mental focus on His Kingdom assignment:

> *2 Fulfil ye my joy, that ye be likeminded, having the same love, being of one accord, of one mind.*
> *3 Let nothing be done through strife or vainglory; but in lowliness of mind let each esteem other better than themselves.*
> *4 Look not every man on his own things, but every man also on the things of others.*
> *5 Let this mind be in you, which was also in Christ Jesus:*
> *6 Who, being in the form of God, thought it not robbery to be equal with God:*

7 But made himself of no reputation, and took upon him the form of a servant, and was made in the likeness of men:
8 And being found in fashion as a man, he humbled himself, and became obedient unto death, even the death of the cross.
9 Wherefore God also hath highly exalted him, and given him a name which is above every name:
10 That at the name of Jesus every knee should bow, of things in heaven, and things in earth, and things under the earth;
11 And that every tongue should confess that Jesus Christ is Lord, to the glory of God the Father.
12 Wherefore, my beloved, as ye have always obeyed, not as in my presence only, but now much more in my absence, work out your own salvation with fear and trembling.
13 For it is God which worketh in you both to will and to do of his good pleasure. (Philippians 2:2-13)

Jesus had a fixed and confident mind. He concentrated on executing His divine assignment instead of contemplating the possibility of failure. He did not waver or allow thoughts of fear or intimidation to stop Him. No matter the challenges He faced, He always resolved to do the will of His Father. And because of His determination, He fulfilled His purpose as Savior of the world. Jesus was successful in His mission because He maintained a Kingdom state of mind. We should learn from the way Jesus focused His thoughts on Kingdom priorities.

Let us go back to the example of the elevator. When you ride an elevator with a view of the surrounding city, the higher the elevator rises, the greater the vantage point. The size and shape of the city changes. The cars, businesses, and people on the ground appear smaller, but the view of the landscape as a whole is much grander. You can see a complete picture of the city, not just the individual details.

If we think of the view of the city in relationship to God's Kingdom, then we can conclude that the more we elevate our thinking, the more our thoughts will be captivated by the "bigger picture." We will mature in our Kingdom nature and experience a change in our perspective on life. Like Jesus, we will be less concerned with inconsequential issues and less distracted by negative and debilitating thoughts. Instead, our thoughts, energy, and efforts will focus on what is most important: achieving our purpose as Kingdom Citizens.

KINGDOM REFLECTION

The Kingdom of God is available to transform our lives. This transformation is possible through the renewal of our minds and the elevation of our thinking. Renewing the mind requires us to immerse ourselves in the Word of God and to exchange negative, ungodly, and unproductive thoughts with thoughts that reflect King Jesus and His Kingdom. As you work toward renewing your mind, I encourage you to remember: 1) It is never too late to change your way of thinking, 2) Renewing the mind begins with earnestly **learning from Jesus**, and 3) Your actions will be evidence of your elevated thinking.

When we **learn from Jesus** and follow His example of maintaining a Kingdom state of mind, our thoughts and actions will be in harmony with our Creator's Word, will, and desires.

KINGDOM CHALLENGE

Make a note of one or more areas in your life where you would like to experience transformation and elevation. The Word of God will activate the elevation of your thoughts and perspectives. The result of that elevation will be your transformation. Research scriptures to build your faith and renew your thinking in that area. The process may be challenging, but as you nurture your mind with the Word, your thoughts will empower you to lead a life that is Kingdom focused, peaceful, and pleasing to God:

> *Finally, brothers and sisters, whatever is true, whatever is nole, whatever is right, whatever is pure, whatever is lovely, whatever is admirable—if anything is excellent or praiseworthy—think about such things. (Philippians 4:8 NIV).*

Chapter 8
LEARNING TO MANIFEST THE POWER
OF THE KINGDOM

One of Jesus' top priorities before leaving Earth was to ensure His follow-ers knew how to exercise their Kingdom power and authority. This power would enable them to do the work of advancing God's Kingdom: teaching the Word, training new Believers to become disciples, healing the sick, helping those in need, and overcoming tribulations.

Like the disciples, we too can manifest Kingdom power in our lives. God plants the seed of His Kingdom inside each of us when we are reborn with His Spirit. This seed has limitless potential for Kingdom power to be re-leased in our lives:

> *7 But we have this treasure in earthen vessels, that the excellency of the power may be of God, and not of us. (2 Corinthians 4:7)*

> *31 Another parable put he forth unto them, saying, The kingdom of heaven is like to a grain of mustard seed, which a man took, and sowed in his field:*
> *32 Which indeed is the least of all seeds: but when it is grown, it is the greatest among herbs, and becometh a tree, so that the birds of the air come and lodge in the branches thereof. (Matthew 13:31-32)*

You may be wondering, *"What does it mean to possess and manifest Kingdom power?" "What exactly do I have the power to do?"* Certainly, we cannot walk into a government agency and proclaim that the region is un-der Kingdom rule. People would think we were mad! However, the power of the Kingdom gives us the authority over any circumstance in our lives.

When we access and manifest Kingdom power, our lives will be examples of the Kingdom's existence and its effectiveness.

In this chapter, we will learn:

- How Kingdom power can help us to live out our purpose and maximize the potential of our gifts
- How to triumph over poverty and be productive stewards with our resources
- How to be proactive in overcoming challenges and formulating solutions to problems

EMBRACING KINGDOM PURPOSE

I define Kingdom purpose as God's intention for our existence. Our gifts are the tools we use to carry out that purpose. When we discover our gifts and connect to our purpose, our lives begin to make sense. We come to understand that we are not required to perform vain, religious tasks and activities. Our lives take on more meaning as we use our gifts and talents to serve the advancement of the Kingdom.

Unfortunately, some Believers do not realize their significance in the Kingdom. Either they have not *discovered* God's purpose for their lives, or they have not *embraced* God's purpose for their lives. Those who have not discovered their purpose may have been misguided by parents, leaders, or their own ambitions, and pursued paths that God never intended for them. They may need to communicate with the Lord to reveal the best use of their gifts and to guide them to the path of their purpose.

Those who have not embraced their purpose may be afraid to surrender their lives to the work of the Kingdom, or they may believe that certain types of gifts and talents receive more human rewards and recognition. They pursue goals and involve themselves in activities that they *think* will garner the validation and praise of people. What they do not understand is that ALL gifts, talents, and functions have value in the Kingdom:

> *14 For the kingdom of heaven is as a man travelling into a far country, who called his own servants, and delivered unto them his goods.*

15 And unto one he gave five talents, to another two, and to another one; to every man according to his several ability; and straightway took his journey.
(Matthew 25:14-15)

4 For as we have many members in one body, and all members have not the same office:
5 So we, being many, are one body in Christ, and every one members one of another.
6 Having then gifts differing according to the grace that is given to us, whether prophecy, let us prophesy according to the proportion of faith;
7 Or ministry, let us wait on our ministering: or he that teacheth, on teaching;
8 Or he that exhorteth, on exhortation: he that giveth, let him do it with simplicity; he that ruleth, with diligence; he that sheweth mercy, with cheerfulness. (Romans 12:4-8)

11 And he gave some, apostles; and some, prophets; and some, evangelists; and some, pastors and teachers;
12 For the perfecting of the saints, for the work of the ministry, for the edifying of the body of Christ. (Ephesians 4:11-12)

Many years ago, I had the opportunity to serve with a brother in the faith. He once shared with me that he greatly admired two very popular preachers: Evangelist Jimmy Swaggart and Dr. Oral Roberts. He was very impressed with Evangelist Swaggart's preaching style: the powerful way that he spoke and the effortless and lively way that he moved the podium to articulate his message. He was also in awe of Dr. Robert's ministry to heal the sick. Ultimately, this brother wanted to be a fusion of both preachers: a healer and a dynamic speaker.

He was so in awe of Evangelist Swaggart and Dr. Roberts that he once tried to imitate both preachers during a Sunday morning service. He tried to preach with the flair of Evangelist Swaggart and reproduce Dr. Robert's gift of healing. To his shock, the congregation did not respond to his sermon. Even worse, there was no move of God's Spirit. My colleague said he later asked God, *"Why didn't you show up at the service?"* God responded, *"I didn't recognize you!"*

My dear brother had a lightbulb moment: the only way for him to be effective in ministry was to be at peace with the gifts and the purpose that God intended for *his* life. He needed to discover and embrace *his unique* role in the Kingdom instead of trying to imitate others.

A person can only be effective and excel in the role that God designed for *him*. When a person serves in a capacity not suited for his gifts, he could suffer exhaustion, ineffectiveness, and mislead or hurt others. When we try to imitate the gifts and callings of other Kingdom Citizens, we miss opportunities to touch the lives of people that God intended for us to encounter. I am not saying that we should not push ourselves to grow outside of our comfort zones, but there is a difference between expanding one's *zone* and being in the *wrong zone*.

When you buy an appliance from the store, the manufacturer's manual contains information on the product's function and design. The same is true of your purpose. If you want to discover your role in the Kingdom, then you should consult your Creator (the manufacturer) and His Word (the manual). You can seek counsel and direction from well-meaning and loving people, but only the Lord knows the complete vision for your unique design.

Jesus himself had a unique ministry. Whenever He spoke, He used parables to communicate Kingdom principles, which was very effective. But what would have happened if Jesus had tried to mimic the preaching style and presentation of John the Baptist? What if He wore clothing made of camel skin and ate honey and wild locusts like John (**Matthew 3:4**)? Thankfully, Jesus accepted and stayed true to *His* unique approach to ministry.

Jesus was confident, comfortable, and sure of His calling. He did not try to compete or compare His gift and purpose with anyone else's. Because He embraced His calling, He accomplished what God sent *Him* to do on Earth. **Learn from Jesus**: be an original, not a copy!

MAXIMIZING PERSONAL POTENTIAL

On U.S. highways, speed limits range from 65 to 75 miles per hour. However, most manufacturers design cars with the ability to move at speeds of up to 200 miles per hour! Car manufacturers do not restrict drivers from operating their cars at maximum speed; it is the governing traffic laws that set those limits. A vehicle's potential for speed is like our potential in the Kingdom. God created us in His image. He designed us with the capacity to succeed, but sometimes our beliefs and limited thinking hinder us from maximizing our full potential as Believers. Wow!

26 And God said, Let us make man in our image, after our likeness: and let them have dominion over the fish of the sea, and over the fowl of the air, and over the cattle, and over all the earth, and over every creeping thing that creepeth upon the earth.

27 So God created man in his own image, in the image of God created he him; male and female created he them.

28 And God blessed them, and God said unto them, Be fruitful, and multiply, and replenish the earth, and subdue it: and have dominion over the fish of the sea, and over the fowl of the air, and over every living thing that moveth upon the earth. (Genesis 1:26-28)

In reality, there are no limits to what we can achieve. Unfortunately, some people's potential remains untapped because they have not elevated their minds and lack the fruitful mentality of the Kingdom. Not only can a Believer be hindered by his mindset but also by the mindset of his spiritual leader. Some religious-minded leaders try to control their members by restricting their gifts to their congregations. The leaders fill them with fear about using their gifts out in the world. That sort of manipulation causes their members to be stagnant, insecure, and unproductive.

Pastors and ministers who try to control how congregants use their gifts are much like the religious leaders of Jesus' time. They were more concerned with holding the spiritual development of the people hostage to the traditions and rudiments of Judaism than teaching them how to flourish in life and their relationship with God:

5 So the Pharisees and teachers of the law asked Jesus, "Why don't your disciples live according to the tradition of the elders instead of eating their food with defiled hands?"

6 He replied, "Isaiah was right when he prophesied about you hypocrites; as it is written: "'These people honor me with their lips, but their hearts are far from me.

7 They worship me in vain; their teachings are merely human rules.'

8 You have let go of the commands of God and are holding on to human traditions."

9 And he continued, "You have a fine way of setting aside the commands of God in order to observe your own traditions!" (Mark 7:5-9 NIV)

Believers should never allow the religious and manipulative opinions of others to control them. No Believer should ever be afraid to do what God has placed him or her on Earth to do. Every Citizen of the Kingdom should feel free to advance in their gifts, excel in their personal endeavors, and strive for greater spiritual growth. We should be like the Apostle Paul who said, "**I press toward the mark for the prize of the high calling of God in Christ Jesus**" (Philippians 3:14).

Many of us are only scratching the surface of our potential. Why should we settle for 65 miles per hour when we have the capacity to reach 200? We can reach our full potential by **learning from Jesus. Let's go!**

POWER TO TRIUMPH OVER POVERTY

Millions of people around the world live in extreme poverty. Even nations that are rich in resources have citizens who live in impoverished conditions. They do not have access to necessities such as adequate food, water, and shelter. Despite the prevalence of poverty in our world, I have come to bring you good news. When Jesus introduced the Kingdom, He brought solutions for the ills of humanity, even poverty. For the blind, there was sight; for the mute, there was the ability to speak; for those who were lame, there was the ability to walk; for the dead, there was resurrection; and for the poor, there was access to the provisions of God's Kingdom:

> 22 *Then Jesus answering said unto them, Go your way, and tell John what things ye have seen and heard; how that the blind see, the lame walk, the lepers are cleansed, the deaf hear, the dead are raised, to the poor the gospel is preached. (Luke 7:22)*

Jesus came to preach the "gospel" which means *good news*. The good news that He came to proclaim to the poor was that there was a way out of poverty: The Kingdom. Even though Jesus brought the solution to poverty, He said the poor would always be with us (**Mark 14:7**). You may be asking yourself how can that be? In Greek, the word "poor" means "unproductive people." Thus, poverty remains an issue for some people because of their *unproductive mentality* not because God desires for them to be poor.

Many Believers have embraced the religious idea that poverty is a sign of humility; therefore, they accept financial struggle and lack as the permanent condition of their lives. Poverty also persists in some nations because of unjust governments that hinder the economic prosperity of all their citizens. I must say this: even if a Believer lives in a government struggling with economic challenges, the Lord can still prosper and deliver that individual from their hardships. Jesus taught that if Believers would seek the Kingdom *first* that "**all things [would] be added unto [them]**" (**Matthew 6:33**). This scripture does not put conditions on our access to Kingdom resources. God's Kingdom principles apply to us no matter where we are in the world and no matter the system of government where we reside.

In the **Book of Genesis**, Joseph predicted that famine was coming to Egypt and the surrounding nations (**Genesis 41:53-57 NIV**). To prevent His people from being decimated by the famine, the Lord placed Joseph in a position of power as Pharaoh's chief administrator. He then imparted wisdom to Joseph to prepare Egypt to survive the famine by storing food during times of plentiful harvests:

> *53 The seven years of abundance in Egypt came to an end,*
> *54 And the seven years of famine began, just as Joseph had said. There was famine in all the other lands, but in the whole land of Egypt there was food.*
> *55 When all Egypt began to feel the famine, the people cried to Pharaoh for food. Then Pharaoh told all the Egyptians, "Go to Joseph and do what he tells you."*
> *56 When the famine had spread over the whole country, Joseph opened all the storehouses and sold grain to the Egyptians, for the famine was severe throughout Egypt.*
> *57 And all the world came to Egypt to buy grain from Joseph, because the famine was severe everywhere.*

Had it not been for the vision and wisdom that God gave Joseph, Egypt and the surrounding nations would not have survived.

Imagine how the world would change if the leaders of our time were like Joseph and made decisions based on Godly wisdom? Imagine how the lives of the world's citizens would prosper if the leaders understood and practiced Kingdom principles? I believe the Lord's command to Believers to teach the nations (**Matthew 28:19**) was not only for us to reach the hearts of people but to reach the hearts of world leaders.

When the Lord sent Moses to deliver the Children of Israel from Egypt, darkness had fallen over all of Egypt except for the region of Goshen, where the Israelites lived:

> *22 And Moses stretched forth his hand toward heaven; and there was a thick darkness in all the land of Egypt three days:*
> *23 They saw not one another, neither rose any from his place for three days: but all the children of Israel had light in their dwellings. (Exodus 10:22-23)*

The *darkness* in Egypt and the *light* in Goshen are symbolic of the choices before us. We can choose to live in *darkness* and disregard the power, potential, and resources available to us through our Kingdom Citizenship, or we can choose to be *enlightened* and access the wisdom that is available to us to overcome our circumstances—including poverty.

I am grateful to God that poverty does not have to be a permanent condition. No matter our circumstance or the system of government where we reside, applying Kingdom principles and wisdom can help us to elevate our lives to a place of prosperity.

KINGDOM STEWARDSHIP AND PRODUCTIVITY

Each of us has the potential to lead fruitful and prosperous lives. We can awaken our potential by applying Kingdom principles of productivity and good stewardship:

> *18 But remember the Lord your God, for it is he who gives you the ability to produce wealth, and so confirms his covenant, which he swore to your ancestors, as it is today. (Deuteronomy 8:18 NIV)*

Believers possess the power of the Creator who, in **Genesis 1:1**, formed Heaven and Earth by His Words. When we use the power of our words, we can activate our creativity and ingenuity and generate bold ideas that can bring about positive changes in our lives and the world.

Sadly, some people choose not to put forth any effort to improve their circumstances. **Proverbs 24:33-34** illustrates this vividly:

33 A little sleep, a little slumber, a little folding of the hands to rest—
34 And poverty will come on you like a thief and scarcity like an armed
man. (NIV)

I once heard the story of a man who went to visit his Pastor to discuss a very serious matter.

The man said, *"Pastor, I need to have my eyes checked."*
"Why is that?" asked the Pastor. The man responded, *"It has been three months since I've seen any money!"*

Instead of trying to work and change his financial situation, the man chose to wait for a handout. Unfortunately, some of us are like the man. We believe that we are prisoners of our circumstances. We do not consider how we can use our skills and resources to improve our situations. Jesus' life and ministry show us the opposite: that we can lead fruitful and productive lives.

When Jesus began His ministry, He appointed twelve disciples:

> *13 Jesus went up on a mountainside and called to him those he wanted, and they came to him.*
> *14 He appointed twelve that they might be with him and that he might send them out to preach*
> *15 And to have authority to drive out demons.*
> *16 These are the twelve he appointed: Simon (to whom he gave the name Peter),*
> *17 James son of Zebedee and his brother John (to them he gave the name Boanerges, which means "sons of thunder"),*
>
> *18 Andrew, Philip, Bartholomew, Matthew, Thomas, James son of Alphaeus, Thaddaeus, Simon the Zealot*
> *19 And Judas Iscariot, who betrayed him. (Mark 3:13-19 NIV)*

Jesus traveled with the twelve disciples from city to city preaching the Kingdom and serving those in need. Jesus influenced many for the Kingdom and multiplied the number of His disciples:

> *1 After these things the Lord appointed other seventy also, and sent them two and two before his face into every city and place, whither he himself would come. (Luke 10:1)*

Eventually, the work of Jesus and the disciples resulted in the establishment and exponential growth of the Church. Because of Jesus' commitment, countless generations have entered into the Kingdom of God:

41 *Those who accepted his message were baptized, and about three thousand were added to their number that day. (Acts 2:41 NIV)*

4 *But many who heard the message believed; so the number of men who believed grew to about five thousand. (Acts 4:4 NIV)*

That same potential for exponential growth and productivity exists within every Kingdom Believer. God honors, blesses, and increases those who work hard and put forth the effort to be productive with their gifts and abilities. The "Parable of the Talents" reveals this principle:

14 *For the kingdom of heaven is as a man travelling into a far country, who called his own servants, and delivered unto them his goods.*
15 *And unto one he gave five talents, to another two, and to another one; to every man according to his several ability; and straightway took his journey.*
16 *Then he that had received the five talents went and traded with the same, and made them other five talents.*
17 *And likewise he that had received two, he also gained other two.*
18 *But he that had received one went and digged in the earth, and hid his lord's money.*
19 *After a long time the lord of those servants cometh, and reckoneth with them.*
20 *And so he that had received five talents came and brought other five talents, saying, Lord, thou deliveredst unto me five talents: behold, I have gained beside them five talents more.*
21 *His lord said unto him, Well done, thou good and faithful servant: thou hast been faithful over a few things, I will make thee ruler over many things: enter thou into the joy of thy lord.*
22 *He also that had received two talents came and said, Lord, thou deliverest unto me two talents: behold, I have gained two other talents beside them.*
23 *His lord said unto him, Well done, good and faithful servant; thou hast been faithful over a few things, I will make thee ruler over many things: enter thou into the joy of thy lord.*
24 *Then he which had received the one talent came and said, Lord, I knew thee that thou art an hard man, reaping where thou hast not sown, and gathering where thou hast not strawed:*

25 And I was afraid, and went and hid thy talent in the earth: lo, there thou hast that is thine.
26 His lord answered and said unto him, Thou wicked and slothful servant, thou knewest that I reap where I sowed not, and gather where I have not strawed:
27 Thou oughtest therefore to have put my money to the exchangers, and then at my coming I should have received mine own with usury.
28 Take therefore the talent from him, and give it unto him which hath ten talents.
29 For unto every one that hath shall be given, and he shall have abundance: but from him that hath not shall be taken away even that which he hath. (Matthew 25:14-29)

The Master was pleased with the efforts of the servants who demonstrated faith and initiative by investing His money. The servants with two and five talents chose to focus on the earning potential of what the Master gave them. Their investments yielded double the return. Because of their initiative, the Master promoted them to a higher level of responsibility and management.

Unfortunately, the servant given one talent made excuses and hid his Master's talent in the ground. The Master, disappointed by the servant's lack of faith, took the one talent and gave it to the servant who had wisely invested the five talents. The servant with one talent missed the opportunity for promotion because of his fearful and limited mindset. He did not take advantage of the growth potential of what his master had given to *him*.

Some of us have the mentality of the servant with one talent. Because of fear, insecurity, and even laziness, we make the excuse that the one talent is not enough. We believe that we could do more if we had more. We do not see that our one "talent" has infinite potential because it came from an infinite God. We miss the blessings that could result from our talent's proper investment and use. If you struggle to see the value of your gift or talent, ask God to reveal how that gift can be used to expand His Kingdom. Even if you have just one gift, the maximization of that gift can make a significant impact in the world.

Many of us are seeking opportunities for growth and promotion in our lives. This desire is a natural inclination because God commanded us in

Genesis 1:28 to be "**fruitful and multiply.**" Although we want to grow and expand, we may not receive opportunities to do so until we prove that we can be good managers (stewards) of what we currently possess. Jesus says, "**He that is faithful in that which is least is faithful also in much: and he that is unjust in the least is unjust also in much**" (Luke 16:10). God, in His wisdom, gives us time to mature to a level where we can manage greater amounts of responsibility.

In the beginning, God created the Heavens and the Earth. Scripture reveals, "**There was not a man to till the ground**" (Genesis 2:5b). There was only a vapor that humidified the Earth and nourished its seeds. God created man and placed him on Earth to tend to its upkeep. Once man was created, the Earth began to produce. In the **Book of Genesis**, we read, "**And out of the ground made the Lord God to grow every tree that is pleasant to the sight, and good for food**" (Genesis 2:9a).

The same principle applies to our lives. Until God can find responsible people in His Kingdom to use the resources they already possess, He will not send more seeds (resources) or rain (His blessing). Show the Lord that you can be a good steward of the gifts, talents, and resources that He has already given to you. Apply them to the manifestation of your purpose and dreams. Your efforts could translate into increased sources of income, a successful business legacy for your family, or an idea that could positively affect your community.

DOMINION OVER PROBLEMS AND CIRCUMSTANCES

Some of the benefits of possessing Kingdom power are being able to devise Godly solutions to our problems and being able to exercise dominion over our circumstances. Jesus is the greatest problem solver in history. All His miracles attested to His ability to devise solutions to the situations He encountered. Jesus' first miracle involved Him solving a problem at a Wedding in Cana. Due to a miscalculation, the wedding host did not have enough wine for the guests. As you can imagine, this was a serious issue because the wine was a significant part of the celebration. Once the wine ran out, I am sure the host was extremely worried. What would he serve his guests? Mary, Jesus' mother, went to Him for help because she knew He could solve the problem. When Jesus learned that there was no wine, He used His wisdom and power to create a solution. He did not panic nor complain. He had the servants fill empty vessels with water, and He super-naturally transformed the water into wine:

1 On the third day a wedding took place at Cana in Galilee. Jesus' mother was there,
2 And Jesus and his disciples had also been invited to the wedding.
3 When the wine was gone, Jesus' mother said to him, "They have no more wine."
4 "Woman, why do you involve me?" Jesus replied. "My hour has not yet come."
5 His mother said to the servants, "Do whatever he tells you."
6 Nearby stood six stone water jars, the kind used by the Jews for ceremonial washing, each holding from twenty to thirty gallons.
7 Jesus said to the servants, "Fill the jars with water"; so they filled them to the brim.
8 Then he told them, "Now draw some out and take it to the master of the banquet." They did so,
9 And the master of the banquet tasted the water that had been turned into wine. He did not realize where it had come from, though the servants who had drawn the water knew. Then he called the bridegroom aside
10 And said, "Everyone brings out the choice wine first and then the cheaper wine after the guests have had too much to drink; but you have saved the best till now."
11 What Jesus did here in Cana of Galilee was the first of the signs through which he revealed his glory; and his disciples believed in him.
(John 2:1-11 NIV)

We must **learn from Jesus** and use our God-given wisdom to find solutions to the challenges we face.

How many people can truly say that they have heard teachings that empower them to respond to dilemmas with a proactive attitude? So often in religious settings, leaders teach people to respond to difficulties with prayer *alone*. Unfortunately, some rely on prayer as a passive response so that they do not have to take responsibility for their circumstances.

Some ministries with national and international influence also seem to encourage people to take a passive approach toward life's challenges. Many radio and television programs promise to pray for their audiences. Thousands of people, crying out for solutions for very serious issues, send letters and emails to these ministries requesting prayer. Let me pause and say that many organizations legitimately pray for those who request prayer. However, some ministries read very few of those letters or emails. Their main reason for offering prayer is to expand their mailing lists.

I sincerely believe that most people genuinely pray for others, but there are those with a religious attitude who promise to pray as a convenient way to dismiss their brothers and sisters who need help. *"Yes, I am praying for you,"* is a phrase that they automatically use in response to those in need, but it is not a sincere promise. Sadly, an empty promise of prayer can be devastating for people who are accustomed to relying on the prayers of others.

Thankfully, this is not the way of the Kingdom. Prayer should not be an excuse to abandon our responsibility in a situation. The Kingdom does not teach us to run and request prayer from others at the first sign of a problem. The Kingdom encourages us to act within our power and with the guidance of the Word. There are times when prayer, in agreement with other Believers, can inspire a solution. But when we pray on our own, we should be confident that the answers we seek will come from God who lives within us. The Word of God says, **"For the Lord giveth wisdom: out of his mouth cometh knowledge and understanding"** (Proverbs 2:6).

PRAY BUT HAMMER AWAY

For so long, many churches have encouraged a "pray only mentality" instead of a mentality of putting faith into action. In the past, Believers may have learned to pray and wait, but the Kingdom of God empowers us to act **NOW**. There is a popular saying in Argentina, *"Go ahead and pray, but hammer away."* In other words, it is good to pray, but we should also make sure that we have done all that is within our power to change our situations. God is not pleased with those who are idle. He prefers that we pray without abandoning action.

There was a man in the Bible who suffered from an illness for thirty-eight years. When Jesus met the man, he was lying near the Pool of Bethesda in Jerusalem. The pool was special because periodically, an angel would come to agitate its water. When the angel visited, whoever entered the pool first would be healed of his disease. Strangely, whenever the angel came to the pool, the man was never able to enter the water in time to receive healing:

1 After this there was a feast of the Jews, and Jesus went up to Jerusalem.
2 Now there is in Jerusalem by the Sheep Gate a pool, which is called in Hebrew, Bethesda, having five porches.
3 In these lay a great multitude of sick people, blind, lame, paralyzed, waiting for the moving of the water.
4 For an angel went down at a certain time into the pool and stirred up the water; then whoever stepped in first, after the stirring of the water, was made well of whatever disease he had.
5 Now a certain man was there who had an infirmity thirty-eight years.
6 When Jesus saw him lying there, and knew that he already had been in that condition a long time, He said to him, "Do you want to be made well?"
7 The sick man answered Him, "Sir, I have no man to put me into the pool when the water is stirred up; but while I am coming, another steps down before me."
8 Jesus said to him, "Rise, take up your bed and walk."
9 And immediately the man was made well, took up his bed, and walked. (John 5:1-9 NKJV)

When Jesus passed by the pool, He lovingly asked the man, *"Do you want to be healed?"* The man responded, *"Sir, I have no one to help me."* Notice the Lord did not ask the man if he had anyone to help him into the pool. He asked the man if he wanted healing. The man's feelings of helplessness nearly interfered with his opportunity to receive healing from Jesus. What did Jesus do with that unfortunate man? He gave Him a word of empowerment: "[**Rise, take up your bed, and walk**]."

When we share our problems with the Lord or discuss them with others, we often use the same excuse as the man: *"I have no one to help me."* And even when the Lord presents a solution to us, if we have become too comfortable in our frailty, we will respond from a place of weakness or discouragement instead of determination. When God speaks regarding our needs, He presents the only answer. We should abandon the habit of making excuses and instead adopt a practice of exercising our faith. It is crucial for God's Children to know that we have access to power to handle our circumstances. When we **learn from Jesus**, we learn how and when to act concerning our circumstances.

I once heard a story of a group of senior women who organized an all-night vigil to pray about the crime in their city. They decided to invite another sister from their community to come and pray with them. The women informed her that they were specifically praying for the authorities to shut down a local hotel used for drugs and prostitution. After hearing the women's prayer focus, the sister said, "I'm out of here!" The women were surprised that she was leaving; they had assumed she was going to pray with them all night.

After they had ended their vigil the next morning, the women noticed that the hotel was on fire. They called the sister at home to tell her the news.

"Our prayers have been answered!" they shouted.

"I know," she said, *"I am the one who set the hotel on fire. You told me what you were praying for, and I took care of it!"*

Please do not try this at home! I am not recommending that you set fire to your community, but I will say that we can certainly learn from the sister's attitude of TAKING ACTION. Sometimes we pray too much instead of using Kingdom principles to bring about a solution. Remember: there is a time to pray and a time to **Hammer Away!**

KINGDOM REFLECTION

Some evidence of Kingdom power at work in our lives may include:

- An increase in our joy and peace
- A stronger sense of personal identity and purpose
- Maximization of our potential
- An increase in our productivity, prosperity, sense of responsibility, and stewardship
- An enhanced ability to solve problems

1. Manifesting Kingdom power means we understand that God has given us the resources, skills, and abilities to meet the demands of life, but we must choose to believe, access, and act with what He has given us. When we **learn from Jesus'** example of manifesting Kingdom power, we can understand our level of responsibility in managing situations and how to apply a proper balance of prayer and action. Through prayer and action, we can do great works for the Kingdom:

11 Believe me that I am in the Father, and the Father in me: or else believe me for the very works' sake.

12 Verily, verily, I say unto you, He that believeth on me, the works that I do shall he do also; and greater works than these shall he do; because I go unto my Father. (John 14:11-12)

KINGDOM CHALLENGE

Embracing Your Kingdom Purpose

God created each of us with unique gifts and talents for a specific purpose. If you have struggled to identify your purpose or struggled to understand the value of your gifts, you should ask God to reveal His purpose for your life and its value to His Kingdom:

4 The word of the Lord came to me, saying,
5 "Before I formed you in the womb I knew you, before you were born I set you apart; I appointed you as a prophet to the nations." (Jeremiah 1:4-5 NIV)

13 For you created my inmost being; you knit me together in my mother's womb.
14 I praise you because I am fearfully and wonderfully made; your works are wonderful, I know that full well. (Psalm 139:13-14 NIV)

Maximizing Your Potential and Productivity

Has God inspired you to use your gifts to achieve a specific dream or vision? Write down the vision and ask God to give you the wisdom to develop a plan of action. When you invest time, hard work, and faith in that plan, your dreams and goals will come to fruition:

The plans of the diligent lead to profit as surely as haste leads to poverty. (Proverbs 21:5 NIV)

Dominion Over Circumstances

Do you want more confidence to face life's challenges? I encourage you to develop your "dominion" muscles through prayer, wisdom, and proper action. God has given you the power to triumph and live like a mighty Citizen of the Kingdom:

37 No, in all these things we are more than conquerors through him who loved us.

38 For I am convinced that neither death nor life, neither angels nor demons, neither the present nor the future, nor any powers,

39 Neither height nor depth, nor anything else in all creation, will be able to separate us from the love of God that is in Christ Jesus our Lord. (Romans 8:37-39 NIV)

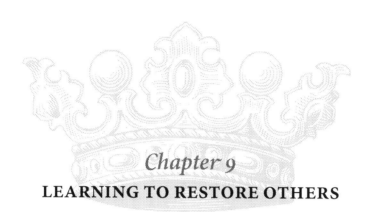

Chapter 9
LEARNING TO RESTORE OTHERS

The news media has a history of reporting stories on people who have made terrible mistakes in their careers and personal lives. Every day, a new scandal is revealed involving someone in a position of prominence. The press rarely invests the same effort in restoring an individual's reputation as they invest in exposing their mistakes. And unfortunately, it is extremely difficult for those who are at the center of the scandal to recover their good name.

We not only see this phenomenon in the media but also in the context of everyday life. How often do we participate in the decline of someone's reputation by perpetuating negative gossip about them? How often do we see the failure of our neighbors, brothers, or sisters, and take steps to restore them back to their original position of respectability, trust, and integrity? Do we make any effort to help repair and rebuild not just the public image, but the self-image and inner being of those who have fallen?

Believers typically use the term *restoration* in regards to a person's reputation. However, the main intent of restoration is to restore a person's joy, peace, and assurance in God. The Apostle Paul teaches, **"For the kingdom of God is not a matter of eating and drinking, but of righteousness, peace and joy in the Holy Spirit"**(Romans 14:17 NIV).

I have included this chapter in the book because forgiveness, redemption, and liberty were hallmarks of Jesus' ministry. If we are serious about **learning from Jesus**, then we should learn to practice His method of loving, restoring, and leading people to the Kingdom no matter their mistakes.

In this chapter, we will learn:

- Jesus' approach to restoration
- The true meaning of repentance and restoration
- Guidance for Believers on how to restore others

THE IMPORTANCE OF RESTORATION TO JESUS

Jesus' primary mission on Earth was to restore man's relationship with God and to restore man's place in the Kingdom. There are many examples of Jesus offering forgiveness, mercy, and complete restoration to those He encountered. One powerful example is the account of a woman with an immoral reputation who wanted to honor Jesus:

> *37 A woman in that town who lived a sinful life learned that Jesus was eating at the Pharisee's house, so she came there with an alabaster jar of perfume.*
> *38 As she stood behind him at his feet weeping, she began to wet his feet with her tears. Then she wiped them with her hair, kissed them and poured perfume on them.*
>
> *44 Then he turned toward the woman and said to Simon, "Do you see this woman? I came into your house. You did not give me any water for my feet, but she wet my feet with her tears and wiped them with her hair.*
> *45 You did not give me a kiss, but this woman, from the time I entered, has not stopped kissing my feet.*
> *46 You did not put oil on my head, but she has poured perfume on my feet.*
> *47 Therefore, I tell you, her many sins have been forgiven—as her great love has shown. But whoever has been forgiven little loves little.*
> *48 Then Jesus said to her, "Your sins are forgiven."*
> *(Luke 7:37-38, 44-48 NIV)*

The woman's kindness moved Jesus, so He showed her great compassion and mercy. What was equally phenomenal, Jesus forgave and honored the woman in the presence of religious leaders who had likely judged, condemned, and shunned her. Can you imagine how much this woman's life changed because of Jesus' gifts of forgiveness and restoration? She received complete freedom from the guilt and shame of her mistakes; restoration of her public image; and assurance that Jesus had accepted her act of love and repentance. Just like Jesus restored the woman, we can help those who are seeking freedom from shame and guilt to find restoration, wholeness, and a renewed life in the Kingdom of God. Let us continue to **learn from Jesus** and be available to help restore others.

KEYS FOR RESTORATION

Some would argue that it can be very difficult to help restore someone who has made a mistake. We may limit our interactions with them and exclude them from our social circles, organizations, and even church activities. Some of us are only willing to restore people based on the nature of their mistakes. And when we do restore them, it is often with conditions. Depending on the amount of pain and suffering they have caused, we may not give them the position, title, or place of prominence that they once occupied.

Although the world may have difficulty restoring those who have committed a fault, the Word of God gives Believers guidance on how to deal with our brothers and sisters who need to recover from damaging situations:

> 1 *Brothers and sisters, if someone is caught in a sin, you who live by the Spirit should restore that person gently. But watch yourselves, or you also may be tempted.*
> 2 *Carry each other's burdens, and in this way you will fulfill the law of Christ.*
> 3 *If anyone thinks they are something when they are not, they deceive themselves.*
> 4 *Each one should test their own actions. Then they can take pride in themselves alone, without comparing themselves to someone else,*
> 5 *For each one should carry their own load.*
> 6 *Nevertheless, the one who receives instruction in the word should share all good things with their instructor. (Galatians 6:1-6 NIV)*

Leading someone through a process of restoration should be done with gentleness and Godly wisdom. I would like to suggest that we keep in mind the following guidance when restoring our brothers, sisters, and friends:

1. Remember Our Imperfections – When we consider our challenges, it allows us to empathize with and show mercy to those who have made decisions due to poor choices and personal struggles with wrong thinking or destructive habits:

1 "Do not judge, or you too will be judged.
2 For in the same way you judge others, you will be judged, and with the measure you use, it will be measured to you.
3 "Why do you look at the speck of sawdust in your brother's eye and pay no attention to the plank in your own eye?
4 How can you say to your brother, 'Let me take the speck out of your eye, when all the time there is a plank in your own eye?
5 You hypocrite, first take the plank out of your own eye, and then you will see clearly to remove the speck from your brother's eye."
(Matthew 7:1-5 NIV)

There is a passage in the Bible in which a group of religious leaders caught a woman in adultery. Because of their legalistic attitudes, they wanted to stone her. Instead of agreeing with their harsh sentence, Jesus posed a merciful and wise argument on the matter:

3 Then the scribes and Pharisees brought to Him a woman caught in adultery. And when they had set her in the midst,
4 they said to Him, "Teacher, this woman was caught in adultery, in the very act.
5 Now Moses, in the law, commanded us that such should be stoned. But what do You say?"
6 This they said, testing Him, that they might have something of which to accuse Him. But Jesus stooped down and wrote on the ground with His finger, as though He did not hear.
7 So when they continued asking Him, He raised Himself up and said to them, "He who is without sin among you, let him throw a stone at her first." (John 8:3-7 NKJV)

After Jesus had challenged their "moral authority" to stone the woman, He stooped down and began to write on the ground with His finger. The Scripture is not specific about what Jesus wrote, but it does say that the men dropped their stones on the ground. They walked away from the incident utterly ashamed and convicted by their conscience:

8 And again He stooped down and wrote on the ground.
9 Then those who heard it, being convicted by their conscience, went out one by one, beginning with the oldest even to the last. And Jesus was left alone, and the woman standing in the midst.
10 When Jesus had raised Himself up and saw no one but the woman, He said to her, "Woman, where are those accusers of yours? Has no one condemned you?"

*11 She said, "No one, Lord." And Jesus said to her, "Neither do I con-
demn you; go and sin no more." (John 8:8-11 NKJV)*

Jesus' response to the teachers and Pharisees reminds me of the saying, *"People who live in glass houses should not throw stones."* We are all vulnerable to criticism because of our past mistakes and imperfections. The Word of God testifies that none of us can stand in our own sense of morality because we all have faults. The Apostle Paul teaches in the **Book of Romans, "For all have sinned, and come short of the glory of God"** (Romans 3:23). The only righteousness that a Believer can claim to possess is that which he received by accepting the power of the resurrected Christ.

Considering that we all have imperfections, we should think about how we would want our brothers and sisters to deal with us if they were to catch us in a delicate matter. Would we want them to throw stones and condemn us, or would we want them to extend us mercy just as Jesus had extended to the woman caught in adultery?

2. Understand the True Process of Repentance – Many believe "repentance" means that an individual feels guilt about his or her mistakes. Some people also assume that repentance should occur instantly or overnight. But the meaning and process of repentance is far more profound and takes time. Repentance means to turn away from harmful thinking or behavior and return to an elevated spiritual place. Repentance should inspire us to change our thinking and behavior so that they reflect our positions as Children of God and representatives of His Kingdom.

Even after a person has repented for their mistakes, people with a religious attitude may still look to accuse and condemn the person for his or her actions. They may scrutinize the individual's conduct because they do not see the change that has taken place in the person's heart. Just because they cannot see the changes with the visible eye does not mean that the individual has not made peace with God. The Lord forgives the same moment that a person confesses, repents, and makes a genuine commitment to change their thinking and ways:

*9 If you declare with your mouth, "Jesus is Lord," and believe in your
heart that God raised him from the dead, you will be saved.
10 For it is with your heart that you believe and are justified, and it is
with your mouth that you profess your faith and are saved.*

11 As Scripture says, "Anyone who believes in him will never be put to shame."
12 For there is no difference between Jew and Gentile—the same Lord is Lord of all and richly blesses all who call on him,
13 For, "Everyone who calls on the name of the Lord will be saved."
(Romans 10:9-13 NIV)

Those of us who understand the value of God's forgiveness and mercy must not only support our brothers and sisters through their process of repentance, but each of us should also take our moments of repentance seriously. Please do not be mistaken, Jesus' willingness to forgive does not give us permission to do whatever we like or to take advantage of God's grace. We may face many temptations and may even fall along the way, but we must continue to try our best to live in a manner that pleases God and always consider the potential consequences of our actions:

16 For a just man falleth seven times, and riseth up again: but the wicked shall fall into mischief.
17 Rejoice not when thine enemy falleth, and let not thine heart be glad when he stumbleth:
18 Lest the Lord see it, and it displease him, and he turn away his wrath from him. (Proverbs 24:16-18)

24 The sins of some are obvious, reaching the place of judgment ahead of them; the sins of others trail behind them.
25 In the same way, good deeds are obvious, and even those that are not obvious cannot remain hidden forever. (I Timothy 5:24-25 NIV)

Our physical bodies may still have issues and want to fulfill desires that are not in harmony with the Spirit of God. However, if we continue to feed our souls with the Word of God, our souls will be so strong that we will be able to overcome those desires, and we will gain wisdom on how to avoid situations that could cause us to stumble:

15 I do not understand what I do. For what I want to do I do not do, but what I hate I do.
16 And if I do what I do not want to do, I agree that the law is good.
17 As it is, it is no longer I myself who do it, but it is sin living in me.
18 For I know that good itself does not dwell in me, that is, in my sinful nature. For I have the desire to do what is good, but I cannot carry it out.

19 For I do not do the good I want to do, but the evil I do not want to do—this I keep on doing.
20 Now if I do what I do not want to do, it is no longer I who do it, but it is sin living in me that does it. (Romans 7:15-20 NIV)

11 And he gave some, apostles; and some, prophets; and some, evangelists; and some, pastors and teachers;
12 For the perfecting of the saints, for the work of the ministry, for the edifying of the body of Christ. (Ephesians 4:11-12)

Unfortunately, the problem with some of us is that we enthusiastically embrace the teachings of the Kingdom for a season, but when living a transformed life becomes difficult, our faith gives out, we become frustrated, and we backslide to our old ways. Let us encourage one another not to give up or consider ourselves as failures. Instead of sliding backward, we should *slide forward to the Kingdom.*

3. Accept God's Forgiveness of Others – When restoring our brothers and sisters, we must accept that they have received God's forgiveness. If we look at our brothers and sisters with spiritual eyes, then we can acknowledge that anyone who believes in Jesus' sacrifice for humanity is perfect. By perfect, I am referring to their spirit. His or her spirit is righteous and holy in the sight of God. Sin and imperfection are no longer barriers to their connection to God. All the person's faults are forgiven, and his spirit is without stain or blemish. The body may have imperfections, but the inner man (the Spirit) is now pure. God does not see the person in the shadow of their mistakes; He sees them in the light of His forgiveness. Do you realize the magnitude of this miracle?

7 The law of the Lord is perfect, refreshing the soul. (Psalm 19:7a NIV)

1 Therefore, since we have been justified through faith, we have peace with God through our Lord Jesus Christ,
2 Through whom we have gained access by faith into this grace in which we now stand. And we boast in the hope of the glory of God. (Romans 5:1-2 NIV)

20 I have been crucified with Christ and I no longer live, but Christ lives in me. The life I now live in the body, I live by faith in the Son of God, who loved me and gave himself for me. (Galatians 2:20 NIV)

4. Restore Without Condemning – When we condemn others, we permanently mark and judge them based on their actions. Usually, when we judge others, we are only assessing what we see on the surface. That sort of judgment might be acceptable in human justice systems, but in God's Kingdom, it is not our place to judge the actions of others. Jesus sees beyond what is external. He knows everyone's thoughts and the motives that influence our decisions:

> *1 "Do not judge, or you too will be judged.*
> *2 For in the same way you judge others, you will be judged, and with the measure you use, it will be measured to you.*
> *3 "Why do you look at the speck of sawdust in your brother's eye and pay no attention to the plank in your own eye?*
> *4 How can you say to your brother, 'Let me take the speck out of your eye,' when all the time there is a plank in your own eye?*
> *5 You hypocrite, first take the plank out of your own eye, and then you will see clearly to remove the speck from your brother's eye.*
> *(Matthew 7:1-5 NIV)*

The Lord says that if we are part of His Kingdom, then we are to be mature in dealing with those who have stumbled or who are walking down a different path. We should be humble in our effort to guide them to the path of the Kingdom:

> *19 My brothers and sisters, if one of you should wander from the truth and someone should bring that person back,*
> *20 Remember this: Whoever turns a sinner from the error of their way will save them from death and cover over a multitude of sins (James 5:19-20 NIV).*

> *2 Carry each other's burdens, and in this way you will fulfill the law of Christ.*
> *3 If anyone thinks they are something when they are not, they deceive themselves.*
> *4 Each one should test their own actions. Then they can take pride in themselves alone, without comparing themselves to someone else,*
> *5 For each one should carry their own load. (Galatians 6:2-5 NIV)*

God is very clear in His Word on this matter of restoring without condemning. Condemnation does a person more harm than good. *Restoration loses its meaning if we injure the person who has done wrong.*

Restoration of a brother or sister calls for spiritual maturity. Ironically, when a brother or sister falls, it not only reveals his or her weakness but also the level of spiritual maturity of those who seek to restore that person. Not everyone has the maturity to help someone who has fallen. Many should refrain from trying because they may end up doing greater harm, especially those who have a religious mindset. The language of a religious person tends to be very harsh and judgmental: *"Get ready,"* they say, *"the wrong you have done is going to cost you dearly. The consequences of your mistakes are inevitable. You will be punished."* That kind of language and approach does not please God. We should learn from the words of Jesus when He said to the woman caught in adultery, **"Neither do I condemn you; go and sin no more"** (John 8:11b NKJV).

The Apostle Paul emphasized to the churches in Galatia that those who restore others should be "spiritual" **(Galatians 6:1 NIV)**. A spiritual man says to the one who committed the fault: *"You were misled, you made a mistake, but you are still a child of God. God is still your Father. God loves you, but He will not approve wrong behavior. God expects you to grow up and be a mature person in the Kingdom."*

I must also shed light on another matter. Some of us may not be mature enough to restore another person because we lack discretion. When we restore someone, we should not share that person's issues with others. We should take that person's trusted confession to the grave! Discretion is a sign of a mature minister of God.

If you have conquered challenges in the past, if you are mature in the Word and rooted in Kingdom teachings, if you understand how Jesus dealt with those who made mistakes, and you know how to love without condemning, then you should make yourself available to support your brothers or sisters when they fall.

5. Restoration is an Act of Love – Restoring without condemning requires us to act from a place of love. Love is what enabled Jesus to forgive those He encountered:

> 28 And one of the scribes came, and having heard them reasoning together, and perceiving that he had answered them well, asked him, Which is the first commandment of all?
> 29 And Jesus answered him, The first of all commandments is, Hear, O Israel; The Lord our God is one Lord:

30 And thou shalt love the Lord thy God with all thy heart, and with all thy soul, and with all thy mind, and with all thy strength: this is the first commandment.
31 And the second is like, namely this, Thou shalt love thy neighbour as thyself. There is none other commandment greater than these.
(Mark 12:28-31)

20 If a man say, I love God, and hateth his brother, he is a liar: for he that loveth not his brother whom he hath seen, how can he love God whom he hath not seen? (I John 4:20)

Our love for others should lead us to protect rather than expose those who have made a mistake. The Apostle Peter, in his First Epistle to Believers of the early Church, states, **"And above all things have fervent love for one another, for "love will cover a multitude of sins"** (1 Peter 4:8 NKJV).

Love does not look for opportunities to badger or remind a person of their mistakes. Instead, love sees beyond a person's mistakes and allows the individual to have a fresh start. The **Book of 1 Corinthians**, which contains one of the greatest passages on the characteristics of Love, states, **"It does not dishonor others, it is not self-seeking, it is not easily angered, it keeps no record of wrongs"** (1 Corinthians 13:5 NIV).

Love is the fuel that will empower us to show compassion and extend support to our brothers and sisters when they stumble. Love will give us the wisdom to guide them gently to the path of the Kingdom. Let us **learn from Jesus'** compassion and mercy toward those who falter. Let us learn from the righteousness and love that He demonstrated while on Earth. Jesus teaches that to love God and to be sensitive to the needs of others is to fulfill the greatest commandment found in Scripture:

37 Jesus said unto him, Thou shalt love the Lord thy God with all thy heart, and with all thy soul, and with all thy mind.
38 This is the first and great commandment.
39 And the second is like unto it, Thou shalt love thy neighbour as thyself. (Matthew 22:37-39)

KINGDOM REFLECTION

Jesus is our example of how to restore our brothers and sisters. He always showed compassion and love to those who needed forgiveness. When faced with the opportunity to condemn someone for his or her mistakes, we must remember the instances when God forgave and restored us. We should also recognize that we are all vulnerable to the same temptations as our brothers and sisters. Their struggles should stir a deep sense of compassion within us.

As we support our brothers and sisters through their time of restoration, we must engage them with a spirit of humility by keeping in mind our journey of repenting from ways that were not pleasing to God. We also need to value the grace that God shows us by not reverting to our old ways. Mature Kingdom Citizens do not take for granted that we are holy, perfect, and righteous because of Jesus Christ alone!

KINGDOM CHALLENGE

How do you typically respond to those who make mistakes? How do you respond to yourself? Ask God to show you how to be compassionate when you or others stumble:

> 12 Speak and act as those who are going to be judged by the law that gives freedom,
> 13 Because judgment without mercy will be shown to anyone who has not been merciful. Mercy triumphs over judgment. (James 2:12-13 NIV)

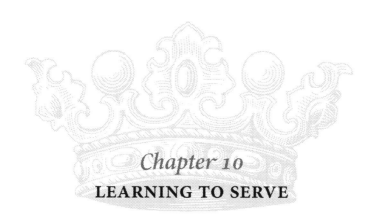

Chapter 10
LEARNING TO SERVE

One of the greatest lessons we can **learn from Jesus** is to serve humanity. Heaven rewards us when we serve with the right motives and when we show generosity to others.

In this chapter, we will learn:

- How to serve others with our gifts and possessions
- How to serve others with the message of the Kingdom
- How to serve with a Godly attitude and with the right motive

JESUS: THE GREATEST SERVANT

The Son of God left Heaven and came to Earth to offer man a better existence. He could have stayed in Heaven while humanity languished in its separation from God. Instead, He chose to come and sacrifice His life so that all God's creation could experience the beauty of being part of His Kingdom. Essentially, the Son of God left Heaven *to serve* humanity:

27 And whosoever will be chief among you, let him be your servant:
28 Even as the Son of man came not to be ministered unto, but to minister, and to give his life a ransom for many. (Matthew 20:27-28)

5 Let this mind be in you, which was also in Christ Jesus:
6 Who, being in the form of God, thought it not robbery to be equal with God:
7 But made himself of no reputation, and took upon him the form of a servant, and was made in the likeness of men. (Philippians 2:5-7)

In our commitment to **learning from Jesus**, we should follow His example of serving those who are in need. Jesus teaches, **"Take my yoke upon you and learn from me, for I am gentle and humble in heart, and you will find rest for your souls"** (Matthew 11:29 NIV). Because Jesus is no longer physically on Earth, those of us who are Believers are encouraged to function as His Earthly representatives. Therefore, if someone needs to see a reflection of Jesus' love and compassion for humanity, then that person should be able to look at the attitudes and actions of Believers.

Ambassadors of the Kingdom represent the interests of the King. For Jesus, *service* holds prime significance. In fact, service is so important to Jesus that He declared it as the way for a disciple to achieve greatness in the Kingdom:

> *25 But Jesus called them unto him, and said, Ye know that the princes of the Gentiles exercise dominion over them, and they that are great exercise authority upon them.*
> *26 But it shall not be so among you: but whosoever will be great among you, let him be your minister;*
> *27And whosoever will be chief among you, let him be your servant:*
> *28 Even as the Son of man came not to be ministered unto, but to minister, and to give his life a ransom for many. (Matthew 20:25-28)*
>
> *46 An argument started among the disciples as to which of them would be the greatest.*
> *47 Jesus, knowing their thoughts, took a little child and had him stand beside him.*
> *48 Then he said to them, "Whoever welcomes this little child in my name welcomes me; and whoever welcomes me welcomes the one who sent me. For it is the one who is least among you all who is the greatest." (Luke 9:46-48 NIV)*

The Scripture is not specific about what sparked the argument between the disciples or why they were competing to be the "greatest" among their group. Jesus addressed the matter, not by discussing each of their merits, but by teaching them the Kingdom's standard of greatness: service to God and their fellow man.

SERVING WITH OUR GIFTS

One of the most exciting benefits of being a Citizen of the Kingdom is that each of us can serve in a unique capacity. God designed every human being with a specific gift or talent that can impact the lives of others. That is why in Chapter 3, *"Learning the Kingdom of God,"* I discussed the importance of each Believer understanding his or her identity and purpose. Knowing who you are and knowing your purpose will help you find ways to serve others.

In *Rediscovering the Kingdom*, Dr. Myles Munroe refers to Kingdom Citizens as servants and kings who are equipped to perform a specific assignment on Earth:

> *The Kingdom of God is the only Kingdom in which every citizen is designated a king. Their rulership is not over people, but a specific area of gifting. This is why Jesus is referred to as the King of kings and Lord of lords. We are kings who serve the world with our God-given gift.*[1]

A Citizen of God's Kingdom is significant not because he possesses a certain title or a particular gift, but because God entrusted that person to use his gifts to lead others to the Kingdom. Every role in the Kingdom has value. Sometimes we may make the mistake of comparing or assigning levels of importance to certain gifts in the Kingdom. The truth of the matter is, we can all be #1 in the Kingdom by excelling at what God has assigned each of us to do and using our gifts to benefit the lives of others.

SERVING WITH THE RIGHT MOTIVE

During His ministry, Jesus made it a point to declare that He came to Earth to do the will of His Father. His motive for helping people was not to make a name for Himself nor to advance a personal agenda; instead, it was to fulfill His purpose of restoring the Kingdom of God on Earth.

When Jesus performed miracles, He would instruct those that He helped not to draw attention to the incident. He desired to obey the will of God and to ascribe all glory to His Father. One notable example of this is the story of Jairus, a ruler of the Synagogue whose daughter had fallen ill. Jairus went to Jesus to request healing for his daughter, but she died while he and Jesus were on the way to his home. When they finally arrived, a crowd greeted them. I am sure they expected Jesus to heal the girl publicly; however, Jesus did the exact opposite. He chose to handle the matter behind closed doors instead of in the public eye:

> 49 While Jesus was still speaking, someone came from the house of Jairus, the synagogue leader. "Your daughter is dead," he said. "Don't bother the teacher anymore."
> 50 Hearing this, Jesus said to Jairus, "Don't be afraid; just believe, and she will be healed."
> 51 When he arrived at the house of Jairus, he did not let anyone go in with him except Peter, John and James, and the child's father and mother.
> 52 Meanwhile, all the people were wailing and mourning for her. "Stop wailing," Jesus said. "She is not dead but asleep." (Luke 8:49-52 NIV)

Jesus restricted the number of people who could come into the house because He was only concerned with serving the needs of the family. He had no interest in entertaining and impressing the crowd with His power.

Luke 8:55-56 confirms that Jesus' only motivation was to do the will of His Father concerning the child and her family:

> 55 Her spirit returned, and at once she stood up. Then Jesus told them to give her something to eat.
> 56 Her parents were astonished, but he ordered them not to tell anyone what had happened. (NIV)

Notice what Jesus did after the child woke up: He commanded the parents to feed the child. He also told them not to discuss her healing with anyone. Jesus' attention was 100% focused on the child's well-being. He could have gone outside to the crowd and announced, *"I performed the miracle; I raised her from the dead! And by the way, I am the Son of God."* Jesus could have had an attitude of self-importance, but He refused to exploit the opportunity to boast of Himself. The purpose of the miracle was to fulfill the will of God and bring glory to His Father.

If that same incident were to occur in modern times, the scenario would be completely different. Imagine for a moment that someone brought a child with a terminal illness to church for prayer. What would happen if we were to pray and the child received a miracle of healing? What is the first thing that we would do? In today's society, because we are so accustomed to publicizing anything extraordinary, we would probably contact every news and social media outlet to announce the miracle to the entire world. We would say, "Let's call a press conference so the child can give her testimony!" But what would happen to the child? Would we abandon her needs and give our attention to promoting and exploiting the miracle? In the presence of such a great phenomenon, would the child's welfare take second place?

We need to be aware of what matters to Jesus. Our motivation to serve should not be to receive the praise of people but to uplift others. When we choose to promote and publicize our works to gain validation from others, it is a sign that we do not know who we are in the Kingdom and that we do not recognize the value of our service in the eyes of God:

> *10 As every man hath received the gift, even so minister the same one to another, as good stewards of the manifold grace of God.*
> *11 If any man speak, let him speak as the oracles of God; if any man minister, let him do it as of the ability which God giveth: that God in all things may be glorified through Jesus Christ, to whom be praise and dominion for ever and ever. Amen. (I Peter 4:10-11)*

We must ask ourselves if our goal is to dedicate our gifts in service to the Lord or our self-interest. Like Jesus, our ultimate motivation for service should not be to gain popularity or distinction in the eyes of men, but rather to use our gifts to honor God and help others. The Word of God encourages us, **"And whatsoever ye do in word or deed, do all in the name of the Lord Jesus, giving thanks to God and the Father by Him"** (Colossians 3:17). Let us **learn from Jesus** and serve with the right motives.

SERVING THROUGH OUR MESSAGE

Jesus' great commission to the disciples was for them to take the message of the Kingdom to the world. Even after His resurrection, Jesus stressed to His disciples—and Peter specifically—the importance of sharing His words with others:

> *15 When they had finished eating, Jesus said to Simon Peter, "Simon son of John, do you love me more than these?"*
> *"Yes, Lord," he said, "you know that I love you."*
> *Jesus said, "Feed my lambs."*

16 Again Jesus said, "Simon son of John, do you love me?"
He answered, "Yes, Lord, you know that I love you."
Jesus said, "Take care of my sheep."
17 The third time he said to him, "Simon son of John, do you love me?"
Peter was hurt because Jesus asked him the third time, "Do you love me?" He said, "Lord, you know all things; you know that I love you."
Jesus said, "Feed my sheep." (John 21:15-17 NIV)

There are countless people in the world searching for a more meaningful existence. They know that there is more to life, but they do not know how to begin the process of changing their lives. Kingdom Citizens can help lead those who are lost to the profound truths of the Kingdom.

When people approach us for answers to life's questions, we should be ready to offer them Jesus' teachings on the Kingdom. The Apostle Paul encouraged us to be prepared to share our knowledge of Jesus with others when he said, **"Study to shew thyself approved unto God, a workman that needeth not to be ashamed, rightly dividing the word of truth"** (2 Timothy 2:15).

If you discipline yourself every day to study the Word of God, you will be prepared to share the surest path to personal enlightenment: **The Kingdom of God.**

Years ago, there was a young man with a drug problem who came to me for counseling. He had struggled with his addiction for years, and because of this, many people said he would never overcome it. I decided to take a common-sense approach to counseling him. I told him God created man in His image and that He designed man to dominate. I told him that drugs are fundamentally plants and that he had the power to dominate plants; plants did not have dominion over him. The young man was astonished! He could not believe what I was telling him. He said that no one had ever shown him that perspective of overcoming addiction. His soul responded to my words of encouragement, and he began to make a change. He applied the Word of God and experienced freedom from his addiction!

Anyone who has had a personal encounter with Jesus can go to others and share His comfort, freedom, and salvation. You can say with all authority, *"Come with me, for the Lord is with me. I am going to lead you to a place where you will learn the words and wisdom of Jesus."*

By sharing the teachings of Jesus and the Kingdom, we can be a source of hope to those who are grappling with issues of great spiritual significance and who desire a connection to the Creator. We can give them THE ANSWER: JESUS' MESSAGE.

Our job is to study Jesus' words, learn of their riches, and share them with those who hunger in their souls. That is the Kingdom at work! We should not be comfortable knowing there are people around us who lack revelation of the Kingdom and therefore struggle to improve their lives. We must do something relevant for our brothers and sisters with the teachings we have learned.

When we give people the message of the Kingdom, we can help them envision a better life. The stories, parables, illustrations, and teachings of Jesus are the best lessons that we can present to others. Remember, Jesus said, **"Learn from Me!"**

HELPING THOSE WHO ARE IN NEED

Kingdom Citizens should help those who are in need and empathize with those who suffer: **"As we have therefore opportunity, let us do good unto all men, especially unto them who are of the household of faith"** (Galatians 6:10). Our support and generosity to others can confirm the existence of God and His love for them.

The Apostle James said that true religion should focus on a person's spiritual *and* practical needs:

> *27 Religion that God our Father accepts as pure and faultless is this: to look after orphans and widows in their distress and to keep oneself from being polluted by the world. (James 1:27 NIV)*

The story of Jesus feeding the 4,000 shows us that He considered the needs of the people's souls as well as their bodies. For three days, the men, women, and children had been listening to Jesus teach, so He had great compassion for them. On the last day of His sermon, Jesus multiplied seven small loaves of bread and a few fish so the people could eat and have enough energy for their journey home. He did not allow any of them to go away hungry:

1 In those days the multitude being very great, and having nothing to eat, Jesus called his disciples unto him, and saith unto them,
2 I have compassion on the multitude, because they have now been with me three days, and have nothing to eat:
3 And if I send them away fasting to their own houses, they will faint by the way: for divers of them came from far. (Mark 8:1-3)

In this Scripture, Jesus teaches us the importance of considering people in an integral way. By integral, I mean the needs of the soul (mind and emotions) as well as the needs of the body (food, shelter, clothing, etc.).

Just like Jesus shared the disciples' bread and fish with the 4,000, we should be willing to serve people with our resources and possessions. Our material possessions are not solely for our consumption and pleasure; rather, God blesses us so that we can share with others. If we had to select a passage of Scripture that clearly communicated the Lord's directive for Believers to respond to and share with those in need, it would be the following:

35 For I was hungry and you gave me something to eat, I was thirsty and you gave me something to drink, I was a stranger and you invited me in,
36 I needed clothes and you clothed me, I was sick and you looked after me, I was in prison and you came to visit me.
37 "Then the righteous will answer him, 'Lord, when did we see you hungry and feed you, or thirsty and give you something to drink?
38 When did we see you a stranger and invite you in, or needing clothes and clothe you?
39 When did we see you sick or in prison and go to visit you?'
40 "The King will reply, 'Truly I tell you, whatever you did for one of the least of these brothers and sisters of mine, you did for me.'" (Matthew 25:35-40 NIV)

Some of us may be skeptical of helping others. Perhaps people from our past have taken advantage of our generosity, and we want to protect ourselves from that happening again. This inclination is understandable. There will always be people who seek to take advantage of our kindness, but we can always ask the Lord to give us wisdom for how to help those who come to us. We should not allow the negative intentions of some to hinder us from being a blessing to those who truly need it.

Many times, people have come to my office for help, and I have given them food or money out of my pocket. I imagine that some of them might have used the money to pay for their addictions; however, I will not allow those incidents to prevent me from helping others in the future. I prefer to err on the side of mercy and compassion, not judgment. I do not want to miss any opportunity to help someone in need. When we help others, God **increases** our resources and capacity to give:

> *10 Now he who supplies seed to the sower and bread for food will also supply and increase your store of seed and will enlarge the harvest of your righteousness. (2 Corinthians 9:10 NIV)*

In addition to sharing our possessions, our concern for others should also lead to thoughtful action. Consider the story of the paralyzed man:

> *4 Since they could not get him to Jesus because of the crowd, they made an opening in the roof above Jesus by digging through it and then lowered the mat the man was lying on.*
> *5 When Jesus saw their faith, he said to the paralyzed man, "Son, your sins are forgiven."*
> *6 Now some teachers of the law were sitting there, thinking to themselves,*
> *7 "Why does this fellow talk like that? He's blaspheming! Who can forgive sins but God alone?"*
> *8 Immediately Jesus knew in his spirit that this was what they were thinking in their hearts, and he said to them, "Why are you thinking these things?*
> *9 Which is easier: to say to this paralyzed man, 'Your sins are forgiven,' or to say, 'Get up, take your mat and walk'?*
> *10 But I want you to know that the Son of Man has authority on earth to forgive sins." So he said to the man,*
> *11 "I tell you, get up, take your mat and go home."*
> *12 He got up, took his mat and walked out in full view of them all. This amazed everyone and they praised God, saying, "We have never seen anything like this!" (Mark 2:4-12 NIV)*

Before the man met Jesus, I wonder if any of the religious leaders had done anything to help him? Had they made sure he had food and water each day? Had they attended to any of his needs? The Scripture does not say, but it does reveal that it was because of the active faith of the man's friends that the man was presented to Jesus and ultimately received healing.

Because there was a massive crowd surrounding the home, the man's friends could have decided that it was too difficult to get to Jesus. They could have sat him outside of the home and hoped that Jesus would have seen the man when leaving the house. However, they knew the surest way for their friend to receive healing was to carry him directly into the presence of Jesus. They not only lifted their friend onto the roof but also tore a hole in it so they could lower him into the house! Do you realize how much strength and determination that required?

There are times that we need to be like the man's friends and go the extra mile to help meet the needs of others.

SERVING WITH THE RIGHT ATTITUDE

Service is what you offer with your hands as well as what you do with the right heart. The more you allow the Kingdom to transform your life, the more you will demonstrate a Godly nature. In the **Book of Galatians**, the Apostle Paul refers to the evidence of possessing Godly character as the **Fruit of the Spirit**:

> 22 But the fruit of the Spirit is love, joy, peace, longsuffering, gentleness, goodness, faith,
> 23 Meekness, temperance: against such there is no law. (Galatians 5:22-23)

Our very demeanor and attitude can affect others. Perhaps the world has been unkind to them, and they need to know that God loves and values them. They may need to "feed" from our joy, our longsuffering, and our patience. Demonstrating the fruit of love, joy, kindness, and gentleness can change their lives forever.

How do others feel when they leave your presence? Do they leave feeling rejected? Do they leave your presence sensing the love and acceptance of God? Are you a person that others seek out because of the fruit you bear, or do people tend to run from you because of your bad attitude?

As Kingdom Citizens, our everyday interactions with people are opportunities to show the love of Jesus, even to those who treat us unkindly. In Argentina, we have a saying for people who make unkind or disparaging statements about us. We say, *"They are throwing dirt on me."* Well, in the Kingdom, when someone, *"throws dirt,"* on us, it is an opportunity for us to grow. Instead of feeling defeated by the negativity of others, we should allow ourselves to be a seed of the Kingdom. When we find ourselves covered in dirt (the insults and offenses of others), we should choose to grow, break through that dirt, and become a tree that bears Godly fruit. We should learn to forgive those who hurt us. The teachings and example of Jesus can change our way of thinking and our attitudes so we can respond correctly to those who mistreat us. The fruit that we bear will be a blessing to our lives and others.

THE REWARDS OF SERVICE

God is very clear in His Word that He rewards those who are committed to serving others. The primary rewards of service are joy, peace, and satisfaction in our souls:

> *25 Jesus called them together and said, "You know that the rulers of the Gentiles lord it over them, and their high officials exercise authority over them.*
> *26 Not so with you. Instead, whoever wants to become great among you must be your servant,*
> *27 And whoever wants to be first must be your slave—*
> *28 Just as the Son of Man did not come to be served, but to serve, and to give his life as a ransom for many." (Matthew 20:25-28 NIV)*

> *26 Whoever serves me must follow me; and where I am, my servant also will be. My Father will honor the one who serves me. (John 12:26 NIV)*

> *58 Therefore, my dear brothers and sisters, stand firm. Let nothing move you. Always give yourselves fully to the work of the Lord, because you know that your labor in the Lord is not in vain. (I Corinthians 15:58 NIV)*

In addition to spiritual blessings, the Lord also provides us with tangible rewards for our service to the Kingdom. It can bring about prosperity in our lives. By prosperity, I am not only referring to material riches; I am referring to the integral well-being of our lives—the prosperity of the mind, soul, family, relationships, and finances:

> *8 And God is able to bless you abundantly, so that in all things at all times, having all that you need, you will abound in every good work.*
> *9 As it is written: "They have freely scattered their gifts to the poor; their righteousness endures forever."*

10 Now he who supplies seed to the sower and bread for food will also supply and increase your store of seed and will enlarge the harvest of your righteousness.
11 You will be enriched in every way so that you can be generous on every occasion, and through us your generosity will result in thanksgiving to God. (2 Corinthians 9:8-11 NIV)

Ultimately, our desire to serve should be greater than our desire for a reward. Even Jesus confirmed that serving others was more fulfilling than receiving personal benefits.

35 In everything I did, I showed you that by this kind of hard work we must help the weak, remembering the words the Lord Jesus himself said: 'It is more blessed to give than to receive.' (Acts 20:35 NIV)

If you want to be great in the Kingdom, serve. If you want increased joy and satisfaction in your life, then consider the fruit that you bear. Choose to serve others with your gifts and with a spirit of cheer. You will find fulfillment because of the good that you do in the world.

KINGDOM REFLECTION

Jesus teaches Believers to measure true greatness by our willingness to serve others. As Kingdom Citizens, we should always be prepared to serve. Not only can we serve others by sharing our unique gifts, resources, and the Kingdom message but also by displaying a Godly attitude. When we are willing, prepared, and passionately involved in service, we active Kingdom principles that bring spiritual and tangible rewards into our lives.

KINGDOM ACTION

Believers should not focus on influencing others to serve us, rather, we should seek opportunities to be of service. I encourage you to find ways to serve family members, co-workers, and people in your community. Ask the Lord to reveal to you how you can effectively use your life to bless and enhance the lives of others:

1 *"Take heed that you do not do your charitable deeds before men, to be seen by them. Otherwise you have no reward from your Father in heaven.*
2 *Therefore, when you do a charitable deed, do not sound a trumpet before you as the hypocrites do in the synagogues and in the streets, that they may have glory from men. Assuredly, I say to you, they have their reward.*
3 *But when you do a charitable deed, do not let your left hand know what your right hand is doing,*
4 *That your charitable deed may be in secret; and your Father who sees in secret will Himself reward you openly." (Matthew 6:1-4 NKJV)*

4 *There are different kinds of gifts, but the same Spirit distributes them.*
5 *There are different kinds of service, but the same Lord.*
6 *There are different kinds of working, but in all of them and in every-one it is the same God at work. (I Corinthians 12:4-6 NIV)*

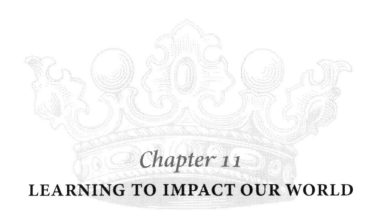

Chapter 11
LEARNING TO IMPACT OUR WORLD

Jesus' impact on the world is immeasurable. He successfully fulfilled His mission to reinstate man's Kingdom birthright and access to God, the Father. The world was never the same after experiencing Jesus' revolutionary ministry:

> *16 For God so loved the world, that he gave his only begotten Son, that whosoever believeth in him should not perish, but have everlasting life. 17 For God sent not his Son into the world to condemn the world; but that the world through him might be saved. (John 3:16-17)*

Just as Jesus dedicated His time on Earth to advancing the Kingdom of God, we as Citizens can leave a mark on the world by continuing His Kingdom work.

In this chapter, we will learn:

- How to apply Kingdom principles to bring about positive changes in our families, communities and nations
- How to promote unity within our society
- How to influence future generations with the Kingdom message

A KINGDOM FOR ALL: PROMOTING UNITY

Throughout history, people have had conflicts over political, economic, and religious ideologies. These disputes have even led to wars that have lasted for generations. Despite mankind's disagreements, hostilities, and divisions, Jesus came to Earth to bring reconciliation and unity. He came to reconcile humanity to God and to reconcile men and women to one another in the Kingdom:

> 20 "My prayer is not for them alone. I pray also for those who will believe in me through their message,
> 21 That all of them may be one, Father, just as you are in me and I am in you. May they also be in us so that the world may believe that you have sent me.
> 22 I have given them the glory that you gave me, that they may be one as we are one—
> 23 I in them and you in me—so that they may be brought to complete unity. Then the world will know that you sent me and have loved them even as you have loved me." (John 17:20-23 NIV)

When Jesus came to Earth, several groups had religious and ethnic disagreements. The Jews did not worship with Samaritans nor did they associate or worship with other non-Jews. The Pharisees and Sadducees (the religious leaders of that time) also had doctrinal divisions and debates. Jesus did not allow cultural, ethnic, or religious disputes to influence His ministry. Instead, He focused on bringing people together into the fold of His Kingdom. *Jesus did not promote discrimination or religion; He promoted invitation and access to the Kingdom:*

> 18 All this is from God, who reconciled us to himself through Christ and gave us the ministry of reconciliation:
> 19 That God was reconciling the world to himself in Christ, not counting people's sins against them. And he has committed to us the message of reconciliation.
> 20 We are therefore Christ's ambassadors, as though God were making his appeal through us. We implore you on Christ's behalf: Be reconciled to God. (2 Corinthians 5:18-20 NIV)

Unlike certain systems of man, there is no discrimination—racial, gender, economic, or otherwise—in the Kingdom of God. **Every** benefit of the Kingdom—whether wealth, education, health, or dominion—is available to ALL its Citizens who live by its principles.

When the Apostle Paul taught the Jews about the Gentiles' equality in Jesus, it sparked much discussion. They did not understand that the Kingdom did not encourage people to embrace prejudiced attitudes. The Jews were perplexed that Paul included the Gentiles in God's plan of salvation because they considered themselves as God's elect (because they were descendants of Abraham). However, Paul taught that Jesus erased the dividing lines when He introduced the Kingdom. Salvation was available for all:

> *28 Be it known therefore unto you, that the salvation of God is sent unto the Gentiles, and that they will hear it.*
> *29 And when he had said these words, the Jews departed, and had great reasoning among themselves.*
> *30 And Paul dwelt two whole years in his own hired house, and received all that came in unto him,*
> *31 Preaching the kingdom of God, and teaching those things which concern the Lord Jesus Christ, with all confidence, no man forbidding him. (Acts 28:28-31)*

> *28 There is neither Jew nor Gentile, neither slave nor free, nor is there male and female, for you are all one in Christ Jesus. (Galatians 3:28 NIV)*

Just like some of the Jews seemed hesitant to accept Gentiles into the faith, how often do we make distinctions in how we treat people or reject others because of our racial, social, economic, or cultural prejudices? How often do we show certain individuals more honor and esteem because of our personal preferences? What does this type of favoritism and partiality teach the world about the Kingdom of God?

In the Epistle of James, he teaches us to be consistent in how we deal with others:

> *8 If you really keep the royal law found in Scripture, "Love your neighbor as yourself," you are doing right.*
> *9 But if you show favoritism, you sin and are convicted by the law as lawbreakers. (James 2:8-9 NIV)*

A spirit of goodwill should prompt us to treat all people with respect, fairness, and love. Our differences should remind us that God gives every person the opportunity to access His Kingdom:

> *18 For through him we both have access to the Father by one Spirit.*
> *19 Consequently, you are no longer foreigners and strangers, but fellow citizens with God's people and also members of his household. (Ephesians 2:18-19 NIV)*

In **Matthew 7:12**, we find the Golden Rule: the most fundamental principle on how to deal with others:

> 12 *So in everything, do to others what you would have them do to you, for this sums up the Law and the Prophets. (NIV)*

A spirit of unity should prevail among all Believers regardless of our differences:

> 1 *Behold, how good and how pleasant it is for brethren to dwell together in unity! (Psalm 133:1)*

> 10 *Now I beseech you, brethren by the name of our Lord Jesus Christ, that ye all speak the same thing, and that there be no divisions among you; but that ye be perfectly joined together in the same mind and in the same judgment. (1 Corinthians 1:10)*

In God's Kingdom, there is no more Jew, Mexican, Argentinean, Nicaraguan, Dominican or any other nationality. Because of Jesus Christ and His Kingdom, we are all brothers and sisters through Him! Do you realize how practicing the principles of reconciliation and unity could influence society for the better? We could bring about more peace in our communities, an increase in fair business practices, and greater cooperation between the political parties who govern our nations.

How do you see your neighbors in the Kingdom? Do you choose to associate with them or give them a certain level of respect based on their culture, social status, gender, or ethnicity? Do you see everyone as being equal in the Kingdom of God? **Learning from Jesus** means learning to welcome and embrace everyone in the Kingdom.

IMPACTING THE NATIONS

In a world where nations are seeking to usurp, control, and even destroy one another, we as Citizens of the Kingdom can bring blessings to the nations. As we have read in previous chapters, Jesus commanded the disciples to influence the world with the teachings of the Kingdom:

> 19 *Therefore go and make disciples of all nations, baptizing them in the name of the Father and of the Son and of the Holy Spirit,*

20 And teaching them to obey everything I have commanded you. And surely I am with you always, to the very end of the age." (Matthew 28:19-20 NIV)

Many organizations have used this scripture as the foundation for local and international missionary work. And while these organizations have likely been a blessing to many people around the world, I sometimes wonder if their work included sharing the Kingdom message with the people they served.

I say this carefully (because my intention is not to hurt anyone), but I say it with much conviction: we should not continue to invest resources in programs and activities that do not have the objective of teaching the Kingdom.

Jesus' commission to Believers to share the Kingdom message takes priority in our ministry at Centro Diplomático. Our congregation is part of the International Third World Leaders Association (ITWLA). Established by Dr. Myles Munroe, the ITWLA is an association of Believers that focuses on having a worldwide impact by sharing the good news of the Kingdom of God. We endeavor to emphasize the importance of teaching what Jesus taught. We share the opinion that Believers should not continue to support missionary efforts that do not have the goal of sharing the message of the Kingdom.

IMPACTING YOUR WORLD

You may not have the opportunity to be part of an international delegation or mission, but you can have a significant impact on your nation through your prayers, active participation, and application of Kingdom principles. You can pray for your leaders and lawmakers, help to improve your local community and get involved with issues of national importance. If you have a calling to public service and a passion for politics, then why not serve your country in that manner? Some government officials have no awareness of Godly principles of leadership and governance. Imagine the impact that you, a Kingdom Citizen, could have by displaying Kingdom principles while working in an official government capacity. **Proverbs 29:2a** states, **"When the righteous are in authority, the people rejoice."**

If we recall the story of Joseph, we will notice that he is a prime example of a person who used his gifts to serve society. When Pharaoh appointed Joseph as second in command, it was Joseph's God-given gifts of dream interpretation and administration that enabled him to prepare Egypt for a widespread famine. Because of Joseph's connection with God, not only was there enough grain for the citizens of Egypt, there was also enough grain to supply to other nations:

> 55 When all Egypt began to feel the famine, the people cried to Pharaoh for food. Then Pharaoh told all the Egyptians, "Go to Joseph and do what he tells you."
> 56 When the famine had spread over the whole country, Joseph opened all the storehouses and sold grain to the Egyptians, for the famine was severe throughout Egypt.
> 57 And all the world came to Egypt to buy grain from Joseph, because the famine was severe everywhere. (Genesis 41:55-57 NIV)

As I stated in Chapter 8, we would live in a very different world if the heads of nations entered into the Kingdom of God. The citizens of the world would prosper and thrive if the leaders' made decisions based on Kingdom principles. Jesus' command for Believers to share the Kingdom message becomes that much more relevant when we consider how it could change the hearts of those in power and the lives of the people they govern.

We do not have to remain idle or unresponsive to issues of injustice or other social concerns. We should be involved in matters that affect our communities and our nation. Please understand that I am not suggesting that we be combative or disruptive in our involvement, but I am encouraging us to take part. We can apply the wisdom and principles that we have learned from Jesus and use them to bring about peace in our homes, businesses, communities, and nations.

IMPACTING GENERATIONS

Our work in the Kingdom should not only focus on impacting the present generation but also on preparing the next generation of Believers. Many churches have proud family heritages with memberships that date back many generations. Unfortunately, some of those churches have spiritual foundations based on religious dogma instead of principles of the Kingdom of God. They teach strong values for good "Christian" living and focus on the reward of going to Heaven, but they have never introduced their congregations to the concepts of Kingdom Citizenship and the Believer's calling to expand the Kingdom on Earth. Sadly, whole generations have lived without any exposure to knowledge of the Kingdom.

Many ministries have misled people with traditions and religiosity, and that error has had a negative impact on the family legacies of their congregants. Sometimes I feel ashamed of myself for all the years that I neglected to share the message of the Kingdom with my congregation. I hope that I can help to correct the error of past generations and make sure everyone I teach hears the message that Jesus presented—**The Kingdom of God.**

If you want the time you spend on Earth to be significant, then I encourage you to let go of traditional and religious teachings that have no benefit. Even if they are principles that have been passed down to you through many generations of your church or family, please understand that they are powerless if they do not lead you and your family to experience the life God has planned for those who are part of His Kingdom.

TRAINING OUR CHILDREN

Teaching the Kingdom is the only way to raise a generation with a solid spiritual foundation. At Centro Diplomático, I am committed to training children to be young disciples who use their Kingdom knowledge for the betterment of society. That is my life's mission. I do not want to be a minister that entertains people with meetings and events that have little significance. *I want to train, not entertain!*

I will never get tired of emphasizing the truth of the Kingdom to the younger generations. I want young people to be able to recognize the misleading doctrines of those who teach the Word in religious ways or who may try to entice them with beliefs that would cause them to stray from the Kingdom. I thank God for young people who understand the difference between religion and principles of the Kingdom. I thank God for young people who desire to **learn from Jesus** and His message.

Jesus' work on Earth included ministering to the needs of children:

14 Jesus said, "Let the little children come to me, and do not hinder them, for the kingdom of heaven belongs to such as these." (Matthew 19:14 NIV)

4 Fathers, do not exasperate your children; instead, bring them up in the training and instruction of the Lord. (Ephesians 6:4 NIV)

It is never too early or too late to share the Kingdom message with the children in our families and communities. Teaching them Kingdom principles is the greatest investment we can make in their lives.

Some of you who are parents have either been fervently praying for your adult children to *come into* the Kingdom or for your children (who have backslidden) *to return* to the path of the Kingdom. Many of you dedicated your children to the Lord when they were very young, but they may have chosen to go down a different path. I encourage you to be at peace. That son or daughter may temporarily lose interest in serving God, or even consider denying their faith, but you should know that when you dedicated that son or daughter to the Lord, He registered that dedication in Heaven. With holy zeal, God will go after your child simply because of the seeds of the Word that you planted inside his or her heart. When God begins a work, He perfects and completes it:

6 Train up a child in the way he should go: and when he is old, he will not depart from it. (Proverbs 22:6)

6 Being confident of this, that he who began a good work in you will carry it on to completion until the day of Christ Jesus. (Philippians 1:6 NIV)

Some of you who serve the Lord today were in the same position as your children. Perhaps at one time you sat in a church pew and heard the teachings of the Word. In the beginning, you may have mocked or doubted the teachings of God's Word or had the attitude that you were listening to religious, meaningless talk. However, you eventually came to understand that those words contained the seed of Life. And once the seed of the Word germinated in your soul, it caused a hunger and thirst for God. Those same words that you mocked and ignored were the very same words that led you back to Jesus and His Kingdom. The Word of God can do the same for your children.

Parents, keep **learning from Jesus**. Have rest in your souls concerning your sons and daughters. Trust God to keep His promises. If you have trained your children in God's truths, no matter the difficulties they face, they will have the Word of God in their hearts to guide them back to the ways of God and the Kingdom. Do not fear for your children; the Word of God is their best shield of protection.

Jesus is interested in Believers recovering the dominion and abundant life that man lost in the Garden. That includes the influence that we have over our children and youth. We can impact the children in our families and communities by *teaching* the Kingdom and *living* the Kingdom. We should exhibit Kingdom excellence and integrity in all that we do. We need to build homes where the message of the Kingdom is the center and the priority. We need to be respectful of other people's time by being punctual—making sure we arrive on time to Kingdom gatherings with other Believers, business meetings, and our jobs. We need to reach out to the needy, study to go higher in the Word, and give God our best. We need to be a genuine example of the Kingdom. The younger generations are watching us.

If you want your life to have true transcendence, then I encourage you to fervently commit to **learning from Jesus** and His message of the Kingdom. If you want to be a great man or woman, then provide your family with a strong foundation in Kingdom principles and share the Kingdom message with all of the young people in your life. I assure you that you will leave a lasting legacy. **Future generations will be abundantly blessed when we choose to teach our children to learn from Jesus and His Kingdom.**

KINGDOM REFLECTION

We have the power to impact the world around us by sharing the good news of the Kingdom. We can promote unity in the Kingdom by engaging with our brothers and sisters based on the Word of our Creator, not our prejudices and preferences. We can also affect future generations of Believers by giving our children and families a solid foundation in Kingdom principles.

KINGDOM ACTION

As Kingdom Citizens, we can have a positive influence on our families, communities, and nations. We can demonstrate the message of Jesus and principles of the Kingdom in our words, our lifestyle, and our interaction with others. We should be enthusiastic about sharing our testimony as Believers and strive to leave no one outside the abundant life of the Kingdom.

I encourage you to declare your commitment to promoting positive change in society and to sharing your faith with others. Below is a declaration that our congregation made during one of our services. I hope that it will help you stay motivated in your efforts to influence your world for the Kingdom of God.

> *"I want to be someone that will help others at all times. I desire to keep God's principles and laws with me always. I will study. I will prepare myself with the Word. I will help my brother, my community, and anyone that I can reach so that more people will walk in the eternal truth. Cities, communities, states, and nations will be full of the peace, love, truth, and abundance of God's wisdom!"*

Wisdom is the principal thing; Therefore get wisdom.
And in all your getting, get understanding. (Proverbs 4:7 NKJV)

A FINAL WORD OF ENCOURAGEMENT

Dear Reader:

I hope the time you spent reading this book has had a positive impact on your life. I hope the words of King Jesus, **"Learn from Me,"** have become critically important to the focus of your spiritual development. I pray that you can confidently say, *"I learned from the best Teacher of all!"*

I encourage you to continue to seek King Jesus' teachings and to share the wisdom He reveals to you with others. Those who say yes to the teachings of King Jesus will receive the highest recompense: **rest for their souls!**

The first and last message that Jesus preached was that the Kingdom of God and the dominion that He gave to men and women are available. Now that you have reached this final page, I hope you can declare to the four winds:

"I am a better Citizen of the Kingdom of God because I learned from King Jesus. I can do business, I can prosper, I can enjoy good health, and I can live a happy life because it is available to me!"

Learning from King Jesus is a lifelong commitment. I have included a list of my favorite scriptures that have helped me understand and grow in the ways of God's Kingdom.

I pray that God will continue to illuminate you on your journey. See you at the top!

Your Kingdom Friend,
Dr. Walter Koch

SCRIPTURES TO GROW IN KNOWLEDGE AND UNDERSTANDING OF THE KINGDOM OF GOD

Genesis 22:1-14

[1] Some time later God tested Abraham. He said to him, "Abraham!" "Here I am," he replied.
[2] Then God said, "Take your son, your only son, whom you love—Isaac—and go to the region of Moriah. Sacrifice him there as a burnt offering on a mountain I will show you."
[3] Early the next morning Abraham got up and loaded his donkey. He took with him two of his servants and his son Isaac. When he had cut enough wood for the burnt offering, he set out for the place God had told him about. [4] On the third day Abraham looked up and saw the place in the distance. [5] He said to his servants, "Stay here with the donkey while I and the boy go over there. We will worship and then we will come back to you."
[6] Abraham took the wood for the burnt offering and placed it on his son Isaac, and he himself carried the fire and the knife. As the two of them went on together, [7] Isaac spoke up and said to his father Abraham, "Father?" "Yes, my son?" Abraham replied.
"The fire and wood are here," Isaac said, "but where is the lamb for the burnt offering?"
[8] Abraham answered, "God himself will provide the lamb for the burnt offering, my son." And the two of them went on together.
[9] When they reached the place God had told him about, Abraham built an altar there and arranged the wood on it. He bound his son Isaac and laid him on the altar, on top of the wood. [10] Then he reached out his hand and took the knife to slay his son. [11] But the angel of the Lord called out to him from heaven, "Abraham! Abraham!" "Here I am," he replied.

¹² "Do not lay a hand on the boy," he said. "Do not do anything to him. Now I know that you fear God, because you have not withheld from me your son, your only son."
¹³ Abraham looked up and there in a thicket he saw a ram caught by its horns. He went over and took the ram and sacrificed it as a burnt offering instead of his son. ¹⁴ So Abraham called that place The Lord Will Provide. And to this day it is said, "On the mountain of the Lord it will be provided." (NIV)

Jeremiah 18:1-6

¹ This is the word that came to Jeremiah from the Lord: ² "Go down to the potter's house, and there I will give you my message." ³ So I went down to the potter's house, and I saw him working at the wheel. ⁴ But the pot he was shaping from the clay was marred in his hands; so the potter formed it into another pot, shaping it as seemed best to him.
⁵ Then the word of the Lord came to me. ⁶ He said, "Can I not do with you, Israel, as this potter does?" declares the Lord. "Like clay in the hand of the potter, so are you in my hand, Israel. (NIV)

Jeremiah 31:31-34

³¹ "The days are coming," declares the Lord, "when I will make a new covenant with the people of Israel and with the people of Judah. ³² It will not be like the covenant I made with their ancestors when I took them by the hand to lead them out of Egypt, because they broke my covenant, though I was a husband to them," declares the Lord.
³³ "This is the covenant I will make with the people of Israel after that time," declares the Lord. "I will put my law in their minds and write it on their hearts. I will be their God, and they will be my people.
³⁴ No longer will they teach their neighbor, or say to one another, 'Know the Lord,' because they will all know me, from the least of them to the greatest," declares the Lord. "For I will forgive their wickedness and will remember their sins no more." (NIV)

Matthew 6:25-33

²⁵ "Therefore I tell you, do not worry about your life, what you will eat or drink; or about your body, what you will wear. Is not life more than food, and the body more than clothes? ²⁶ Look at the birds of the air; they do

not sow or reap or store away in barns, and yet your heavenly Father feeds them. Are you not much more valuable than they? ²⁷ Can any one of you by worrying add a single hour to your life?

²⁸ "And why do you worry about clothes? See how the flowers of the field grow. They do not labor or spin. ²⁹ Yet I tell you that not even Solomon in all his splendor was dressed like one of these. ³⁰ If that is how God clothes the grass of the field, which is here today and tomorrow is thrown into the fire, will he not much more clothe you—you of little faith? ³¹ So do not worry, saying, 'What shall we eat?' or 'What shall we drink?' or 'What shall we wear?' ³² For the pagans run after all these things, and your heavenly Father knows that you need them. ³³ But seek first his kingdom and his righteousness, and all these things will be given to you as well. (NIV)

Matthew 23:23-26

²³ "Woe to you, teachers of the law and Pharisees, you hypocrites! You give a tenth of your spices—mint, dill and cumin. But you have neglected the more important matters of the law—justice, mercy and faithfulness. You should have practiced the latter, without neglecting the former. ²⁴ You blind guides! You strain out a gnat but swallow a camel.

²⁵ "Woe to you, teachers of the law and Pharisees, you hypocrites! You clean the outside of the cup and dish, but inside they are full of greed and self-indulgence. ²⁶ Blind Pharisee! First clean the inside of the cup and dish, and then the outside also will be clean. (NIV)

Matthew 28:11-15

¹¹ While the women were on their way, some of the guards went into the city and reported to the chief priests everything that had happened.

¹² When the chief priests had met with the elders and devised a plan, they gave the soldiers a large sum of money, ¹³ Telling them, "You are to say, 'His disciples came during the night and stole him away while we were asleep.' ¹⁴ If this report gets to the governor, we will satisfy him and keep you out of trouble." ¹⁵ So the soldiers took the money and did as they were instructed. And this story has been widely circulated among the Jews to this very day. (NIV)

Mark 8:1-9

[1] During those days another large crowd gathered. Since they had nothing to eat, Jesus called his disciples to him and said, [2] "I have compassion for these people; they have already been with me three days and have nothing to eat. [3] If I send them home hungry, they will collapse on the way, because some of them have come a long distance."

[4] His disciples answered, "But where in this remote place can anyone get enough bread to feed them?"

[5] "How many loaves do you have?" Jesus asked.

"Seven," they replied.

[6] He told the crowd to sit down on the ground. When he had taken the seven loaves and given thanks, he broke them and gave them to his disciples to distribute to the people, and they did so. [7] They had a few small fish as well; he gave thanks for them also and told the disciples to distribute them. [8] The people ate and were satisfied. Afterward the disciples picked up seven basketfuls of broken pieces that were left over. [9] About four thousand were present. After he had sent them away. (NIV)

Luke 14:25-33

[25] Large crowds were traveling with Jesus, and turning to them he said:
[26] "If anyone comes to me and does not hate father and mother, wife and children, brothers and sisters—yes, even their own life—such a person cannot be my disciple. [27] And whoever does not carry their cross and follow me cannot be my disciple.

[28] "Suppose one of you wants to build a tower. Won't you first sit down and estimate the cost to see if you have enough money to complete it? [29] For if you lay the foundation and are not able to finish it, everyone who sees it will ridicule you, [30] Saying, 'This person began to build and wasn't able to finish.'
[31] "Or suppose a king is about to go to war against another king. Won't he first sit down and consider whether he is able with ten thousand men to oppose the one coming against him with twenty thousand? [32] If he is not able, he will send a delegation while the other is still a long way off and will ask for terms of peace. [33] In the same way, those of you who do not give up everything you have cannot be my disciples. (NIV)

John 2:1-11

[1]On the third day a wedding took place at Cana in Galilee. Jesus' mother was there, [2]And Jesus and his disciples had also been invited to the wedding.
[3] When the wine was gone, Jesus' mother said to him, "They have no more wine."
[4] "Woman, why do you involve me?" Jesus replied. "My hour has not yet come."
[5] His mother said to the servants, "Do whatever he tells you."
[6] Nearby stood six stone water jars, the kind used by the Jews for ceremonial washing, each holding from twenty to thirty gallons.
[7] Jesus said to the servants, "Fill the jars with water"; so they filled them to the brim.
[8] Then he told them, "Now draw some out and take it to the master of the banquet." They did so,
[9] And the master of the banquet tasted the water that had been turned into wine. He did not realize where it had come from, though the servants who had drawn the water knew. Then he called the bridegroom aside [10] And said, "Everyone brings out the choice wine first and then the cheaper wine after the guests have had too much to drink; but you have saved the best till now."
[11] What Jesus did here in Cana of Galilee was the first of the signs through which he revealed his glory; and his disciples believed in him. (NIV)

John 10:7-10

[7] Therefore Jesus said again, "Very truly I tell you, I am the gate for the sheep. [8] All who have come before me are thieves and robbers, but the sheep have not listened to them. [9] I am the gate; whoever enters through me will be saved. They will come in and go out, and find pasture. [10] The thief comes only to steal and kill and destroy; I have come that they may have life, and have it to the full. (NIV)

ENDNOTES

CHAPTER 3
LEARNING THE KINGDOM OF GOD

1. Myles Munroe, *Rediscovering the Kingdom Expanded Edition* (Shippensburg, PA: Destiny Image, 2010), 138.
2. Myles Munroe, *Rediscovering the Kingdom Expanded Edition* (Shippensburg, PA: Destiny Image, 2010), 146.
3. Myles Munroe, *Rediscovering the Kingdom Expanded Edition* (Shippensburg, PA: Destiny Image, 2010), 72.
4. Myles Munroe, *Rediscovering the Kingdom Expanded Edition* (Shippensburg, PA: Destiny Image, 2010), 73.

CHAPTER 4
LEARNING TO DISTINGUISH THE KINGDOM
OF GOD FROM RELIGION

1. Myles Munroe, *Rediscovering the Kingdom Expanded Edition* (Shippensburg, PA: Destiny Image, 2010), 21.
2. *Life Application Study Bible.* (Carole Stream: Tyndale House Publishers; Grand Rapids: Zondervan, 2005), 1517-1518. Used by permission.
3. *Life Application Study Bible.* Carole Stream: Tyndale House Publishers; Grand Rapids: Zondervan, 2005), 1519. Used by permission.

CHAPTER 6
LEARNING TO TRUST GOD WITH OUR WELL-BEING

1. Myles Munroe, *Rediscovering the Kingdom Expanded Edition* (Shippensburg, PA: Destiny Image, 2010), 71.

CHAPTER 10
LEARNING TO SERVE

1. Myles Munroe, *Rediscovering the Kingdom Expanded Edition* (Shippensburg, PA: Destiny Image, 2010), 175.

Available Soon...

Tired of Religion
There is Something Better

From a Crown of Thorns
to a Royal Crown

The Government
Desired by God

Printed in the United States
By Bookmasters